Bridges Between Nations Series

Fiesta!
Mexico and Central America

A Global Awareness Program for Children in Grades 2-5

by Barbara Linse and Richard Judd

Fearon Teacher Aids
A Division of Frank Schaffer Publications, Inc.

Editorial Director: Virginia L. Murphy

Editors: Marilyn Trow and Sue Mogard

Copyeditor: Lisa Schwimmer

Design: Rose Sheifer

Musical Adaptations for the Songs: Sarah Michael

Cover and Inside Illustration: Eva Mautner

Cover Design: Teena Remer

Production: Rebecca Speakes

This Fearon Teacher Aids product was formerly manufactured and
distributed by American Teaching Aids. Inc., a subsidiary of Silver Burdett
Ginn, and is now manufactured and distributed by Frank Schaffer
Publications, Inc. FEARON, FEARON TEACHER AIDS and the
FEARON balloon logo are marks used under license from Simon & Schuster, Inc.

Fearon Teacher Aids
A Division of Frank Schaffer Publications, Inc.
23740 Hawthorne Boulevard
Torrance, CA 90505-5927

ISBN 0-8224-4232-9

Printed in the United States of America

1.9 8 7 6

Dedication

In memory of Art Linse, who was deeply interested in multicultural education. He loved Mexico and Central America and the people who live there.

About the Authors

Barbara Linse is a Californian with a lifelong interest in the Spanish beginnings of her state. Ms. Linse did undergraduate work in elementary education at San Jose State University and graduate work in Supervision and Elementary School Curriculum at San Francisco State and Stanford University. Ms. Linse lived in Mexico for three years with her husband and twin son and daughter. She has also done extensive study and travel throughout Mexico and Central America. Ms. Linse has been involved in education as a teacher, curriculum consultant, and supervisor of student teachers. She developed and taught Mexican folk culture for elementary school teachers at the University of California. Currently, she delights in sharing her ideas and knowledge with other teachers through her writings.

Richard Judd graduated from Pennsylvania State University with an M. Ed. He completed a B.S. in elementary education at Lock Haven State (University), a teacher-training center in central Pennsylvania. In California, he has completed credential work in the graduate schools of San Francisco State University and at the University of California, Berkeley. Now retired, Mr. Judd worked in elementary education in San Anselmo, California. He was an elementary principal for twenty years. He gave extra time during his administrative duties to boost music and art wherever possible. Mr. Judd specializes in adapting craft skills of other cultures and passes these experiences on to teachers and students in the United States. Mr. Judd and his family have traveled extensively throughout the world studying the arts and he has taken an interest in celebrating cultural differences.

Acknowledgments

We would like to thank Patricia Carballo, principal of the Mexican-Japanese Primary School of Mexico City and a special consultant for this book, and Barbara Poort and Maria Elena Robbins, translators of the Spanish songs.

♥✕♥ CONTENTS ♥✕♥

FIESTA! MEXICO AND CENTRAL AMERICA

Fiesta! Mexico and Central America explores the origins of Mexican and Central American celebrations that have been passed down from generation to generation. The United States borders Mexico and Central America and it is hoped that through hands-on experiences with Mexican and Central American folk and fine art, classical and folk music, dances, and fiestas, children will develop a feel for and appreciation of the Mexican and Central American cultures.

The Mexican and Central American cultures are a rich blend of Native American influences and Spanish traditions and religion. The history of these areas is similar among the countries because of the expansive settlements of the Native American tribes in Mexico and Central America and the common Spanish occupation during colonization. Information associated with religions is given throughout the text to help children understand Mexican and Central American traditions and customs.

NOTE: Many of these activities have strong religious backgrounds. Please take this into consideration while reviewing each section for your curriculum. You may want to send notes home to parents or guardians on this subject.

You are encouraged to supplement this book with information from parents, local businesses, the children, foreign exchange students, and personal travel and experience in these areas. All these resources will help you bring some of the culture of Mexico and Central America to life in your classroom. Invite the children to experience the countries of Mexico, Guatemala, El Salvador, Honduras, Panama, Costa Rica, Belize, and Nicaragua!

Included as a companion to this resource is a cassette tape of the 17 songs in the music section of this guide. Side one of the tape offers the musical arrangements. Side two provides Spanish vocals, plus the music.

ABOUT THE FORMAT

Fiesta! Mexico and Central America is organized into two sections to provide a maximum of flexibility and encourage the infusion and integration of the material into existing curriculums.

SECTION 1: FIESTAS

This section contains a yearly plan of fiesta celebration ideas. Each fiesta is explored fully through Background Information, Enrichment Activities, and Global Awareness questions.

Background Information

Background information sets the stage for understanding the historical significance of each holiday and gives cultural insights into the activities presented.

Possible Instructional Uses:

◆ Divide the class into cooperative-learning groups. Give each group a copy of the background information and go over the information with the class. Then invite the children to work together in their individual groups to plan a dramatic representation of the information.

◆ Make a class timeline of the dates noted in the information. Compare the dates to similar dates of historical significance in the United States.

◆ Share the information with the children and then ask them to discuss the most interesting, unusual, and exciting aspects about the specific holiday.

Enrichment Activities

Diverse enrichment activities invite children to experience the sights, sounds, smells, feelings, and tastes of individual fiestas. The activities bring the history provided in the background information alive. The children are provided hands-on opportunities to enjoy parades, parties, arts and crafts, foods, and music enjoyed in Mexico and Central America.

Possible Instructional Uses:

◆ Invite the children to work together on activities in small cooperative-learning groups. To facilitate the most efficient use of time and materials, groups might work on activities at staggered intervals.

◆ Set up a variety of activities in stations around the classroom for children to visit and participate in as desired.

◆ Integrate *Fiesta! Mexico and Central America* into your present curriculum. Study fractions in math and then invite the children to make Mexican and Central American foods. Study plants in science during

Candlemas (a fiesta celebrating seeds and new growth), or use Mexican and Central American themes as a basis for reading and writing assignments.

◆ Work cooperatively with the music, art, and physical education teachers. (One of the most effective ways of teaching children to work cooperatively is to model that behavior yourself.) Each fiesta celebration is enhanced through the integration of activities with other parts of the curriculum.

Global Awareness

Global awareness questions encourage children to use their skills in critical thinking, values clarification, and comparison. The children are invited to connect with Mexican and Central American children when they think about the infusion of these cultures in the United States. The questions ask children to make direct comparisons of Mexican and Central American fiesta celebrations with similar United States celebrations. Children see the similarities between their own cultures and the Mexican and Central American cultures, and infer cultural influences in their own lives.

Possible Instructional Uses:
◆ Write the questions on an overhead transparency or duplicate the questions for each student. Invite the children to discuss the questions in small cooperative-learning groups.

◆ Encourage the children to write their responses to a particular question and then share their responses together in class during a designated "global awareness" time.

◆ Help the children brainstorm possible responses to each question. Make a class graph of the many ideas generated.

SECTION 2: RESOURCE BANK

This section contains complete instructions for many of the activities introduced in Section 1. The Resource Bank is organized into Arts and Crafts, Foods, Music, Flags, Maps, and Bibliography. Students are encouraged to gather materials, follow the directions, and complete clean-up independently. In this way, the children are given opportunities to be responsible and independent.

Possible Instructional Uses:
◆ Use the resources in conjunction with yearly fiestas or separately, as an easy-to-use resource when one particular activity is needed.

◆ Duplicate and laminate the ideas and use them to set up learning centers in the classroom.

◆ Send copies of the recipes, arts and crafts, or musical instruments home with the children as enrichment-activity packets.

CREATE A MEXICAN AND CENTRAL AMERICAN ATMOSPHERE IN THE CLASSROOM

Set up your classroom in Mexican and Central American style. The following suggestions will provide creative spaces for the children to use while exploring and experiencing the cultures of Mexico and Central America.

Cooking

Provide a permanent space for storing cooking utensils and ingredients within easy reach of the children. Duplicate, laminate, and store the recipes provided in the Resource Bank. This will enable children to set up the necessary items, prepare the food, and complete clean-up with minimal adult supervision. Make sure a place to display recipes is available near the work area.

Arts and Crafts

Label and store the arts and crafts materials listed in the Resource Bank. Duplicate and laminate directions for the crafts and store them near the materials as well. Children may then make favorite items from specific fiestas all year long during independent work times. Display the children's Mexican and Central American creations during the special fiestas or for everyday fun throughout the year!

Music

Display common rhythm instruments and Mexican and Central American music books in a specified area of the classroom. Make tapes, tape players, and head sets available to encourage the children to listen to Mexican and Central American music independently or to use while playing rhythm instruments. Provide a space for copies of songs enjoyed during the fiestas throughout the year, along with the tape of the music. As the children make their own Mexican and Central American instruments, place these in this area as well.

Marketplace

Establish a Mexican and Central American marketplace in the classroom where the children may share Mexican and Central American items brought from home, handmade arts and crafts, and foods with a Mexican and Central American influence. You may even wish to arrange times for the children to buy, sell, or trade items brought from home or crafts made at school.

Creative Writing

Put out writing and drawing materials, such as colored pens, pencils, markers, crayons, and paper of varying weights and colors. Envelopes and stationery might also be helpful. The following suggestions encourage children to express themselves through their writing.

◆ Journal Writing. Encourage the children to record their impressions of what they feel, envision, smell, taste, and hear during their exposure to the Mexican and Central American cultures. The children may enjoy including drawings, poems, and other items collected during the study of each fiesta as well.

◆ Timeline. Make a large class timeline to display in the classroom. Invite children to add information and significant dates along the timeline as they explore Mexican and Central American fiestas. You may wish to use a contrasting color to add significant historical dates for the United States to make comparisons of the histories more clear. Children may also enjoy making individual timelines as the year progresses to compare historical dates with dates of personal significance to them.

◆ Letters. Invite the children to adopt a pen pal from Mexico or a country in Central America for the school year. The following addresses offer this service. Or, children can send letters to family members to tell them about the fiestas they are studying at school. At the end of the year, the children will then have a record of the year's events through the letters sent home.

World Pen Pals
1690 Como Avenue
St. Paul, MN 55108

Worldwide Pen Friends
P. O. Box 39097
Downey, CA 90241

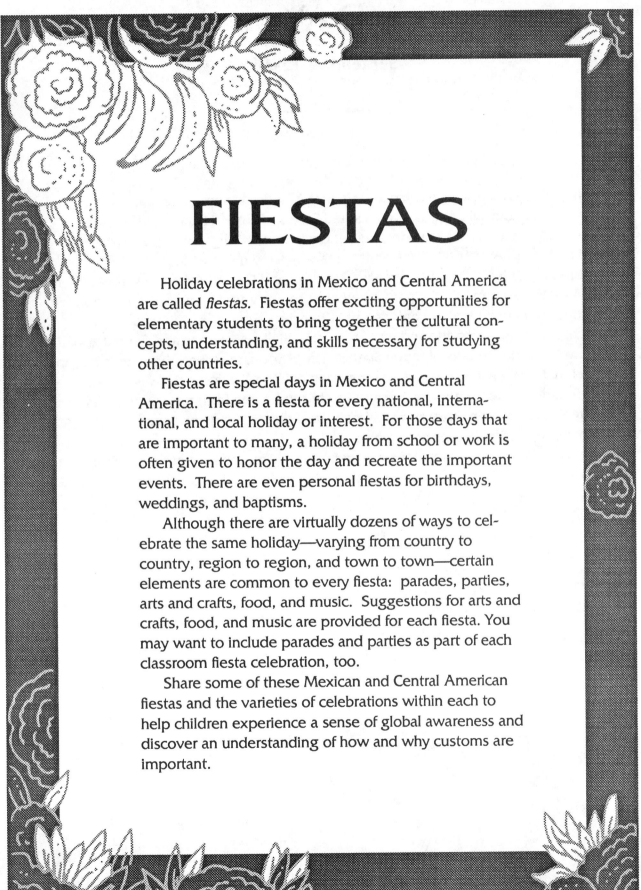

FIESTAS

Holiday celebrations in Mexico and Central America are called *fiestas*. Fiestas offer exciting opportunities for elementary students to bring together the cultural concepts, understanding, and skills necessary for studying other countries.

Fiestas are special days in Mexico and Central America. There is a fiesta for every national, international, and local holiday or interest. For those days that are important to many, a holiday from school or work is often given to honor the day and recreate the important events. There are even personal fiestas for birthdays, weddings, and baptisms.

Although there are virtually dozens of ways to celebrate the same holiday—varying from country to country, region to region, and town to town—certain elements are common to every fiesta: parades, parties, arts and crafts, food, and music. Suggestions for arts and crafts, food, and music are provided for each fiesta. You may want to include parades and parties as part of each classroom fiesta celebration, too.

Share some of these Mexican and Central American fiestas and the varieties of celebrations within each to help children experience a sense of global awareness and discover an understanding of how and why customs are important.

♥✕♥ INDEPENDENCE DAY ♥✕♥

September 15-16

The colonial history of Mexico and Central America is very different from the much shorter colonial periods of the United States. From 1512 to 1821, Mexico, Guatemala, Honduras, El Salvador, Belize, Costa Rica, Nicaragua, and Panama were ruled by Spain. At that time, the entire area was known as Mexico.

Three centuries of Spanish rule gave Mexican and Central Americans little experience in self-government. In Spanish colonies, the king was supreme. He appointed viceroys (governors) to carry out his law. Councils issued laws, supervised the church, and regulated trade and trade routes. Initially, Mexicans and Central Americans were excited and loyal to the Spanish king. Soon, however, the people began to feel that Spain had taken away all their power. The Mexicans and Central Americans felt they were treated unfairly and wanted to be free from the bonds of Spain. Differences of opinion arose and soon people of different regions began to turn against one another as well as Spain.

In the 19th century, most Mexican and Central American countries revolted and became independent republics. In 1810, Father Delores Hidalgo and others decided to cry out, fight, and even die for freedom from Spain. On the afternoon of September 15, the revolution against Spain officially began. Independence was finally gained by 1821. The new independent countries of Central America were formed.

Independence Day is celebrated throughout Mexico and Central America. Mexico, Guatemala, Honduras, El Salvador, Belize, Costa Rica, and Nicaragua celebrate on September 15 with parades and fiestas. Panama gained its independence much later, in 1903, and celebrates its independence in November.

INDEPENDENCE DAY FIESTA

Sponsor an Independence Day Fiesta in your classroom. On September 15, if possible, as the children leave at the end of the day, invite them to shout "Viva Mexico!" as well as names of other countries in Central America. The next day, or on a later day in September, celebrate the Independence. The following ideas will help make this special holiday celebration come alive for the children.

CLASSROOM ENRICHMENT ACTIVITIES

FIESTA INVITATIONS

Help the children make invitations to send to parents and other guests they decide to invite to their class Independence Day fiesta. Children may make the invitations by folding sheets of white construction paper in half and then drawing some of the flags and maps of Mexico and Central American countries on the covers (see pages 232-238). Suggest that children color the covers with crayons, markers, or tempera paint. Inside, the children might write the following:

"Come and help us celebrate the Independence Day of Mexico and Central America. We'll have a parade and everyone will carry a flag."

FREEDOM FIGHTERS BULLETIN BOARD

Title a bulletin board "Freedom Fighters of Mexico and Central America!" Then have the children do independent research to find names, places, and dates that are important to the fight for independence in Mexico and Central America. Suggest that children include pictures that they cut out or draw themselves, titles of songs, and so on.

MEXICAN AND CENTRAL AMERICAN FLAGS

Show the children maps of Mexico and Central America (see pages 237-238). Discuss the countries that make up these regions. Explain that before their independence from Spain, Mexico and Central America were one large country. Enlarge the maps and place them on a bulletin board. Invite the children to make appropriate flags to pin on the countries. Two suggestions are provided here.

1. Divide the class into small cooperative-learning groups. Give each group a copy of one of the flag patterns provided on pages 232-236. Suggest that children research the colors of each flag and then use crayons, tempera paint,

or markers to color the flags. (Encourage the children to research other flags of Central America as well.) Invite the children to pin their flags on the appropriate countries on the map.

2. For flags that really wave, use old white sheets. Enlarge the flag patterns provided on pages 232-236 to the desired size. Then cut the sheeting to fit the patterns. Have the children use crayons to color the flag patterns. Encourage the children to press firmly and color solidly. Then place the sheets over the colored flag patterns. Arrange a layer of newspaper on top, and firmly press an iron over the top of the newspaper to transfer the crayon designs to the sheets. The newspaper layer prevents the crayon from bleeding through. Staple the finished flags to dowel sticks so that children may wave them in their Independence Day parade.

MEXICAN AND CENTRAL AMERICAN MAP

Mexico and Central America were one country until the year 1821. Give each child copies of the outline maps provided on pages 237-238. There are many ways you may use the maps. Encourage the children to research and make a variety of maps—maps to show altitudes, zones, average temperatures, vegetation, products, population patterns, and so on.

FILL-AND-SPILL EGGS

Help the children make fill-and-spill eggs (see page 94). Fill-and-spill eggs are emptied eggshells filled with confetti. A favorite fiesta activity is to crack fill-and-spill eggs above the heads of friends just for fun! Then invite children to shout "¡Viva Mexico!" (or a country in Central America) as they break the eggs open over their friends' heads and enjoy the confetti that spills out.

PAPEL PICADOS

For festive occasions, intricate designs are cut in colored tissue paper to hang as decorations (see pages 120-121). These cut-paper pieces are strung on cords or wires, much like wash on a clothesline.

Divide the class into eight small cooperative-learning groups. Assign one of the countries listed here to each group. Suggest that groups of children make papel picados in the flag colors of their assigned country. The colors of each country's flag are listed here for your convenience.

Mexico	green, white, red
Costa Rica	red, white, blue
Honduras	blue, white
Guatemala	light blue, white
Panama	red, white, blue
El Salvador	blue, white
Belize	red, white, blue
Nicaragua	blue, white

STICK HORSES

There are always toys for Mexican and Central American celebrations. Help the children make stick horses (see pages 137-138) to "ride" in their Independence Day parade. Horses were brought to the Americas by Europeans. There were no horses in Mexico or Central America before Columbus!

WALNUT-SHELL ART

Nutshell art is created all over Mexico and Central America with skillful hands. Real miniature scenes are created in the half-shells using bread dough or chicle art. You can find these miniatures in Mexican and Central American shops in the United States as well. If possible, show the children one of these walnut-shell art pieces. Discuss the skill that would be necessary to make these tiny pieces of art.

Have the children make facsimiles of walnut-shell art by making shoebox dioramas of weddings, bullfights, or other simple Mexican and Central American scenes. Ask children to bring shoeboxes or other types of containers from home. The miniature scenes may be created with paper or clay figures that are then glued into the boxes. Interested children may be challenged to try creating miniature scenes in walnut half-shells!

ALMENDRADO (ALMOND DESSERT)

Almendrado is an especially appropriate patriotic almond dessert to serve for Independence Day (see pages 146-147). It may be made in the colors of a Mexican or Central American country's flag.

FELIZ CUMPLEAÑOS (HAPPY BIRTHDAY)

Feliz Cumpleaños is the Mexican and Central American birthday song (see pages 191-192). It is sung to celebrate the birth of independence in Mexico and Central America and to emphasize the feeling that each person is vitally useful in life. Teach the children the song. Invite the children to sing it for their Independence Day fiesta and then for birthdays now and then throughout the year.

MARACAS

Maracas are easy to make and add a Mexican and Central American beat to any tune. Show the children how to make maracas from balloons (see page 168). Then provide opportunities for the children to play their maracas in their Independence Day parade. They will enjoy playing the maracas for other Mexican and Central American fiestas and other times during the school year as well.

PARAGUAYAN HARP

The Paraguayan gauchos (cowboys) play a simple harp for celebrations or just for relaxation. Although Paraguay is part of South America, this harp is very Mexican and Central American. It is small, has many strings, and is held in the lap while played. Help the children make toy harps to play at their Independence Day celebration (see page 172).

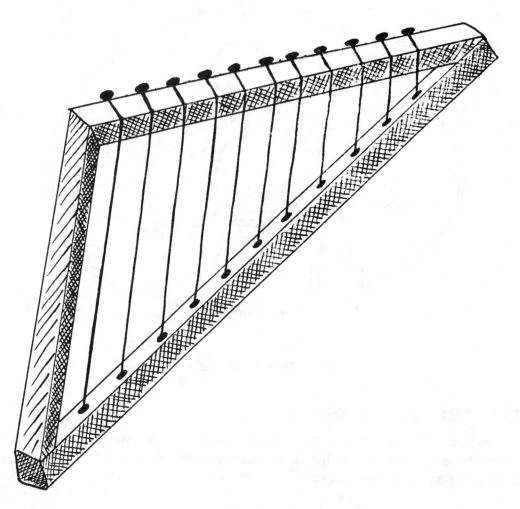

GLOBAL AWARENESS

The following questions will help the children build bridges of understanding between Mexican and Central American cultures and their own cultures.

1. When is Independence Day observed in the United States? How is the Independence Day celebration in the United States similar to the Independence Day celebrations in Mexico and Central America? How are they different?

2. The colors and design of a country's flag tell something about the country the flag represents. Compare the colors and designs of Mexican and Central American flags with the flag of the United States. What does each flag tell you? How are they the same? How are they different?

❤✕❤ DIA DE LA RAZA ❤✕❤

October 12

Before Columbus arrived in America in 1492, all of the Americas were inhabited by Native Americans—the Maya, Aztec, Inca, Huichol, and Cuna. The arrival of Columbus in the Americas in 1492 marked the initial blending of Native American cultures with European cultures. Although Columbus was not the first European to explore this area, he was the first to keep records, return to his sponsoring nation, and give the land to its conqueror, Spain.

Christopher Columbus was born in Genoa, Italy. At the time of his first voyage in 1476, he was only 19 years old. Columbus was intrigued by the stories of the Indies—lands filled with spices, gold, gems, and other beautiful, rich, precious things. But while others traveled to the east to find these exotic lands, Columbus believed he would reach the Indies sooner by sailing west.

On September 12, 1492, he set sail for the Indies with three ships—the *Niña*, the *Pinta*, and the *Santa María*. When he landed in the Bahamas, he thought he was in the Indies. He called all the natives he met there Indians and claimed the land for Spain.

In 1503, after several more voyages, Columbus landed off the coast of Honduras. He claimed this area for Spain as well. He then went to Panama and Costa Rica. Although Columbus didn't colonize Mexico or Central America (Cortez, Pizarro, Balboa, Magellan, and other explorers colonized the new world), he is identified as the first central European to set foot on the Western Hemisphere.

By 1837, the countries of Mexico and Central America had broken away from Spain, but that didn't change the enormous Spanish influence on every aspect of their civilization. Religious practices today are a blending of Catholic and Indian. Native foods are often used with those that originated in Spain. There are many traces of the old mixed with the new. October 12 is observed as a national holiday in most of the Americas. It is called *El Dia de la Raza* (The Day of the Race), celebrating the many racial strands in the history of Mexico and Central America since Columbus' discovery of the Americas. There are usually many fiestas, some lasting several days!

DIA DE LA RAZA FIESTA

Sponsor a Dia de la Raza fiesta in your classroom. The following ideas will help make this special holiday celebration come alive for the children.

CLASSROOM ENRICHMENT ACTIVITIES

AZTEC MARKETS

Share the following story about a Mayan girl at an ancient market with the children. Then invite the children to write possible endings for the story. Suggest that children illustrate their stories as well.

Aztec Market Day

Corn Tassel woke up in the morning. She had been sleeping on a metate, a straw mat. Her mother was slapping tortillas for breakfast. Her family raised corn on the family farm on floating gardens. Her father busily picked corn from the floating garden and loaded it into his boat. It was market day in Mexico City and people were bringing their wares to market in little boats. They had all sorts of wonderful things to sell at the marketplace.

When Corn Tassel and her father reached the marketplace, Corn Tassel looked around. She was drawn to the fragrant smell of beautiful flowers—carnations, clover, and more. The canals were full of boats bringing people and their wares to the marketplace. Some folks were making their goods at the market. They were weaving cloth and making pots to sell. Jewelers were making gold earrings. Little cornbread loaves were cooking on the comal. There were fine turkeys for sale, and gold dust was carried in the turkey feathers. Corn Tassel wished her father had something to sell other than corn.

DISCOVERY PLAY

Share the background information about Columbus and his discovery of America with the children. Help the children write a play about the European discovery of Mexico and Central America. The children may use 3-dimensional sailing ships to help tell the story (see pages 129-130).

AZTEC MARKETPLACE MURAL

The spot where Mexico City stands today was once the capital of the Aztec culture and site of the largest market of Pre-Columbian times. What is known of early Pre-Columbian history and society is based on both conjecture and studies done by archaeologists, anthropologists, historians, and others.

Market Days were about every five to six days and usually held outdoors. Necessities, and some luxuries, were sold, such as shoes, rope, corn, beans, cocoa, peppers, onions, birds, turkeys, rabbits, venison, salt, dyes, paper, frogs, clothes, and even feathers. There were also special market stalls for cooking and stalls that sold fish, fruit, or pottery. Jewelry and furs were sold in the market as well.

Show the children pictures of Mexican markets and the Aztec dressed in native costumes. Share information about Pre-Columbian markets with the children. Then tape a long sheet of butcher paper along one wall in the classroom. Invite the children to paint an Aztec market mural scene (see page 107). As a class, make lists of what to include in the mural. Perhaps the mural might show various craft pieces for sale. Discuss how to make the mural scene seem real—glue feathers on birds or on an Aztec costume, put fur on a bunny or a bear, put jewelry on emperors, add flowers, and so on. Encourage the children to try various mediums—wet chalk, markers, and tempera paint, for example.

CLAY DOLLS

Clay is plentiful throughout Mexico and Central America. Clay is used to make all kinds of toys for Mexican and Central American children. Invite the children to have fun creating dolls from clay (see page 85).

CROSS-STITCH EMBROIDERY

The Huichol Native Americans live in west central Mexico. Their culture dates back through the centuries and has remained quite true to early traditions. Cross-stitch embroidery, a Huichol tradition, dates back to the Maya. The region in which the Huichol live is called *Nayarit*. Nayarit is located in the Sierra Madre Mountains.

The craft ideas of the Huichol people are influenced by plants and animals, such as the peyote plant, rabbits, and deer. Their beliefs focus on such mysteries as death, birth, life, crops that grow and die, as well as the sun and stars.

Invite the children to cross-stitch some designs of their own (see page 88). First, have the children draw their designs on graph paper. Encourage the children to use nature themes in their designs. Then show the children how to cross-stitch their designs on burlap squares. Suggest that children use their finished embroidered squares to decorate purses, belts, and other articles of clothing.

DISCOVERY TELESCOPES

If possible, bring a hand-held telescope to school and invite the children to look through it. Explain to the children that telescopes were not invented during Columbus' time. When Columbus' crew first sighted the Americas, they saw the land with their own eyes. Encourage children to discuss what Columbus and his crew could have seen if they had had a telescope. Point out that now, modern ships have sophisticated computer equipment for navigation.

Provide different sizes of cardboard tubes and paper for the children to make discovery telescopes for their Dia de la Raza fiesta.

GOD'S EYES (OJOS DE DIOSES)

God's eyes are one of the many craft pieces made by the Huichol. They can be simple or complex. Show the children how to make god's eyes (see page 99). Then hang the god's eyes in the classroom as decorations for the Dia de la Raza celebration. Later, invite the children to take their god's eyes home to share with family members.

MOLAS

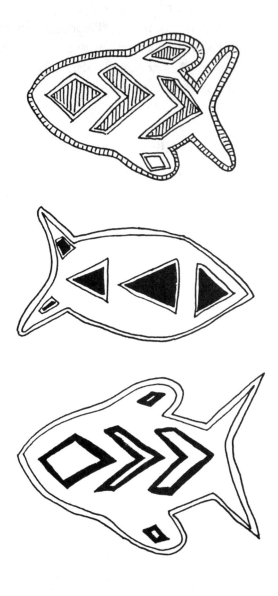

Off the coast of Panama are the San Blas Islands, inhabited by the Cuna Indians. The civilization is old and their crafts have not been significantly modified by outside cultures. The Cuna men fish, hunt a little, and travel by small boats to Panama to earn money for staple goods. The women sometimes spend their days making bright, beautiful molas. Molas are intricate appliques that look extremely complicated and indeed can take weeks to sew. The central design appears to be outlined with a contrasting color. The Cuna women decorate their blouses with molas. They also sell molas to the limited number of tourists who come to the islands.

Invite the children to make paper molas (see pages 104-105). Suggest that the children draw simple designs on various kinds and colors of paper and scrap material. Help the children plan and make visual statements of the animal and plant life that awaited Columbus and his followers. A class applique mural with Mexican and Central American plant and animal life may be started now and continually added to throughout the year, if desired.

NEARIKAS

Huichol men often go on religious pilgrimages into the mountains to enjoy nature. They record the beautiful sights with yarn drawings glued on pieces of wood called *Nearikas*. Invite the children to use these same materials to create beautiful nature drawings (see page 108).

PHONY STONIES

Throughout the centuries, Mexico and Central America were populated by many Native American groups. Artifacts of their cultures are still on the sites they occupied. Sculptures, tombs, huge pictorial frescoes, and bas reliefs are among the many treasures.

Bring in one of nature's best and hardest rocks. Demonstrate what a table knife does to the rock. If carving a soft sculpture takes time, ask the children how long they think it probably took to carve the Pre-Columbian monuments.

Invite the children to make Pre-Columbian monuments from vermiculite or clay for a backdrop for a marketplace. Encourage the children to make carvings to represent each of the four major Pre-Columbian cultures—Olmec, Mayan, Toltec, and Aztec. The differences from the art of one group to another will become very evident as the children carve square corners or round corners, faces, or geometric shapes. This activity is also a fun way to build a Mexican and Central American atmosphere in the classroom.

SAILING SHIPS

If possible, show the children a picture of the ships that Columbus used to sail to the Americas. Help the children compare these ships to modern-day ships. Discuss how long it would probably take to cross the ocean in one of Columbus' ships.

Help the children make 3-dimensional ships like the *Niña, Pinta,* and *Santa María* from folded paper (see pages 129-130). Paper dipped in papier-mâché paste and curved windward make good sails (see page 112).

SPANISH GALLEON PIÑATA

Piñatas are a popular part of most Mexican and Central American celebrations. Make a Spanish galleon piñata following the basic instructions for the frog piñata on pages 126-128, only using a shoebox rather than a clay pot. Fill the piñata with pieces of eight, such as 8 tangerines, 8 gold or silver circles, 8 peanuts, or 8 of whatever you wish. The number eight is special since, in most of Mexico and Central America, the peso is the standard coin. In earlier times, there were eight smaller coins that equaled one peso. The children will have fun trying to break the piñata and sharing the treats that spill out.

WEAVINGS

Weavings from the early Mayan period did not last over time. The textiles rotted in the humid climate. However, it is known from early paintings and carvings that still exist that the early Maya produced beautiful textiles. Textiles were loomed by the people and were often sold in the market. Invite the children to make simple looms on which to weave colorful designs (see pages 143-144). Display the children's finished weavings in the classroom for all to enjoy.

MEXICAN HOT CHOCOLATE

Cinnamon-flavored sweet chocolate was a favorite beverage of the ancient Aztec. Invite the children to make this delicious chocolate drink to serve as a special tribute to the Aztec (see page 158).

SPANISH LUNCH

Ask the children what foods they might pack for a voyage across the ocean. Explain the importance of including foods high in vitamin C. Many sailors suffered from scurvy, a disease caused by a lack of vitamin C in the body. Help the children plan a Spanish lunch for Dia de la Raza. Remind them to include vitamin C to keep the scurvy away!

HAND DRUMS

Music is an important part of every culture. Rhythm instruments have always been a popular way for people to express themselves. Help the children make hand drums (see page 167). Then provide opportunities for the children to accompany Mexican and Central American music with their drums.

GLOBAL AWARENESS

The following questions will help the children build bridges of understanding between Mexican and Central American cultures and their own cultures.

1. Why is Columbus Day observed in the United States? How is this celebration similar to the Mexican and Central American celebration of Dia de la Raza?
2. Peoples of Mexico and Central America are strongly influenced by the Spanish. What cultures are present in your community? How have these cultures influenced your community?
3. What is your favorite part of the Mexican and Central American Dia de la Raza celebration? Why?

 ALL SOULS' DAY

November 2

There are many beautiful, funny, and even some sad celebrations throughout Mexico and Central America. Early in November in Mexico and Central America, the holidays All Souls' Day and All Saints' Day are celebrated. Although these are traditional Catholic holidays, they also coincide with an old Aztec celebration of death.

Part of an early Aztec ritual involved placing food on the graves of the departed. The dead loved one was believed to go on a journey, but stayed close to his or her dear ones. It was believed that the dead came to their graves on November 2 to feast on their favorite foods. It was said that the spirits of the dead only came to take back the fragrance of the food, not the substance, which was later eaten by the living. Tamales were among the delicacies, then as now. Other rites pertaining to death and burial, such as placing flowers on graves, took place in those early times over a period of three days.

With the coming of the Spanish, old Native-American customs mingled with the new. The result was a holiday with absolute uniqueness in arts and crafts, foods, fiestas, and more!

Mexican and Central Americans celebrate All Souls' Day by making ofrendas (little shrines) to place in their homes and in churchyards to honor their loved ones who have died. Families work lovingly to make the ofrendas beautiful. Often, incense and rich yellow or somber black candles are burned. It is believed that the dead love beauty and peek into the living rooms of their families during "holy times" to see the candles and shrines.

Throughout Mexico, where many cultures flow together, death is both respected and feared. Death is common and loved ones are lost frequently. The personalities of the dead loved ones are believed to go on throughout eternity.

There is a particularly beautiful sense among the country people in Mexico and Central America in their communal with the dead. Death is not considered a part of any specific religion. All Souls' Day provides opportunities for the people to honor their departed loved ones.

Note: These activities involve subjects surrounding death. Some children may be sensitive to this issue. Send a note home to parents or guardians before beginning this section on All Souls' Day to explain the purpose of the unit. If, in your judgment, the activities in this lesson may be disturbing to children or parents, you might choose not to use them.

ALL SOULS' DAY FIESTA

Sponsor an All Souls' Day fiesta in your classroom. The following ideas will help make this special holiday celebration come alive for the children.

CLASSROOM ENRICHMENT ACTIVITIES

INVITATIONS TO AN ALL SOULS' DAY FIESTA

Invite the children to make invitations by folding manila paper or other sturdy paper in half. Suggest that children use markers or crayons to draw skeletons on the covers. In Mexico and Central America, skeletons are shown bicycling, wearing big hats filled with loaves of bread, riding horses, dancing, playing the guitar, and getting married, to name a few. White crayon skeletons covered with thin black paint make convincing invitations. Help the children brainstorm some possible titles for the invitations, such as "We feel a party in our bones!" Drawing skeletons for All Soul's Day is a tradition, one celebrated by the culture.

ALFIÑIQUE SKULLS

Foods are very characteristic of cultures. Mexicans and Central Americans shape a sugar-candy mixture, called *alfiñique,* into various shapes to represent the seasons and holidays. At the time of All Souls' Day, it is common to make skulls, skeletons, and bones from alfiñique. These are decorated with pastel frosting. Often, common girls' and boys' names, such as Ricardo, Barbara, Arturo, Carolina, Luis, and Maria, are written in pastel-colored frosting on the top.

Help the children make special alfiñique treats in the shapes of skulls (see pages 78-79). Invite the children to make big candies and little candies. Suggest that they write their initials in frosting on the tops of the candies.

OFRENDAS

Ofrendas are shrines made as Mexican and Central American grave decorations. Religious pieces, beeswax candles, oranges, marigolds, and other native flowers and greenery, such as rose petals and pine needles, are frequently used to decorate the shrines.

Invite the children to make ofrendas from cardboard boxes covered with construction paper (see page 109). Suggest that children sprinkle flower petals carefully around their ofrendas and then place favorite foods nearby. Point out that foods, such as Pan de Muerto (Bread of the Dead) and alfiñique, are very characteristic of Mexican and Central American All Souls' Day celebrations (see pages 148 and 78-79).

MASKS

Help the children make All Souls' Day masks (see pages 117-119). These are papier-mâché masks made to look like skeleton heads. To create the right atmosphere, play an appropriate tape or recording as the children create the masks (see the bibliography provided on pages 239-240). Encourage the children to listen to the skeletons cavort! Then invite the children to wear their masks in their All Souls' Day parade.

PAPER FLOWERS

Mexican and Central Americans sometimes decorate the graves of their loved ones with yellow flowers. Help the children make paper flowers (see pages 95-98). Petal craft is traditional. Often flowers are made much like mosaics, using bits of paper to simulate flower petals. The designs are glued onto cardboard or other sturdy backings.

PAPIER-MÂCHÉ ALL SOULS' DAY FIGURES

There are many figures made in Mexico and Central America to represent All Souls' Day. Skeletons are made from different types of materials. Invite the children to make skeletons and other figures to enhance All Souls' Day from papier-mâché (see pages 114-115). Suggest that the children make prop pieces for the figures as well—perhaps they might show figures riding horses, playing soccer, or doing other activities the children themselves enjoy doing.

SKELETONS

In Guatemala, Honduras, El Salvador, and Mexico, skulls, skeletons, and death and dying were an important part of the cultures of the early agriculturalists—the Maya, Toltec, Aztec, and other classic civilizations.

Invite the children to make a variety of different skeletons to hang in the classroom for decoration. Paper-plate skeletons, paper-tube skeletons, and white coat hangers and rolled paper skeletons are delightful to make (see pages 131-136). Hang the skeletons all over the classroom for the children to enjoy.

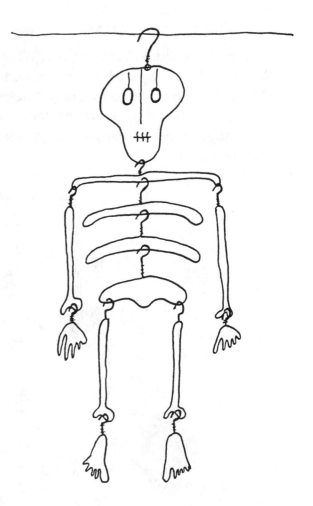

PAN DE MUERTO (BREAD OF THE DEAD)

Throughout Mexico and Central America, decorated bread is made for All Souls' Day. Bread is baked with teardrops and crossbones sculpted on top. The loaves start appearing in bakeries around the middle of October. Pan de Muerto is available in most Mexican bakeries in the United States as well.

Help the children make Pan de Muerto (see page 148). Encourage the children to contribute their favorite bread recipes from home, or use frozen bread dough for convenience. Roll the dough into coils, bake, and you'll have an edible wreath. (The loaves may be sent home for baking, if it is not feasible to bake at school.)

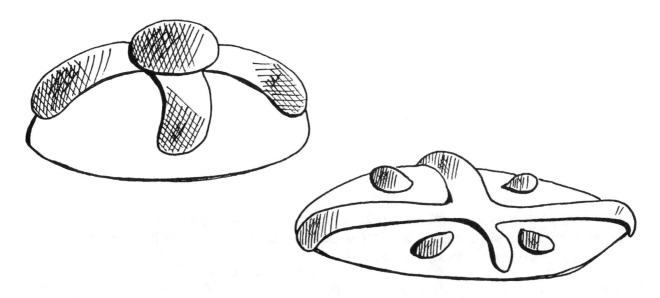

A LA VÍBORA (THE SERPENT)

Teach the children the song *A la Víbora* (see pages 173-174) and then play the following game, a Spanish version of *London Bridge.*

Select two children to role-play gatekeepers under whose arms a line of children must pass as they sing. Have the children caught by the gatekeepers when the music stops form a line behind the gatekeepers. The game continues until all children are caught.

BOX MARACAS

The children will have fun making box maracas (see page 169) to use as noise-makers during their All Souls' Day celebration. Skull shapes may be formed by applying layers of papier-mâché to boxes. When the papier-mâché dries, the children may paint the papier-mâché white. Eyes and mouths may be drawn with black markers once the white paint dries. A few pebbles dropped inside will make interesting sounds when the boxes are shaken.

GLOBAL AWARENESS

The following questions will help the children build bridges of understanding between Mexican and Central American cultures and their own cultures.

1. How are Halloween celebrations different from the All Souls' Day fiestas? In what ways are they similar?

2. All Souls' Day has often been compared to Halloween, but there are many differences. Why is All Souls' Day celebrated in Mexico and Central America? Why is Halloween celebrated in the United States?

3. Most cultures honor their departed loved ones in special ways. Compare and contrast how the dead are honored in the children's cultures.

❤✕❤ DAY OF OUR LADY ❤✕❤ OF GUADALUPE

December 12

The story of Our Lady of Guadalupe begins in 1531 in Mexico. It is said that soon after the conquest of Mexico, Mexico's first Archbishop ordered the destruction of all shrines that the Aztec had painstakingly erected to honor their gods and goddesses. Shortly after the destruction, Juan Diego, a poor young convert, said he saw a vision of Mary, mother of Jesus, on Tepeyac Hill. This had been the site of an Aztec shrine honoring Tonantzeh, the Aztec goddess of earth and corn. Diego's vision of Mary was in the midst of beautiful music and she had a lovely brown face. Mary supposedly told Diego to have the bishop build a church on the spot where she appeared.

The bishop, wanting proof of this vision, asked Juan to have a miracle performed by Mary. As Juan walked home, he was interceded by a friend who told him of the sudden and unexpected recovery of Juan's uncle, who had been very ill. Juan returned to Tepeyac Hill and found roses on the rock where there had previously only been cacti. Juan wrapped the roses in a blue tilma (cape) along with a picture of Mary to show the bishop. The bishop was convinced of a miracle and the chapel was built.

Huge fiestas are held all over Mexico and Central America to honor the Day of Our Lady of Guadalupe. The biggest festival is held at the shrine of Guadalupe itself, just outside Mexico City. People from all over the country come to this shrine annually to get healing water. Aztec dances are performed and a big market is set up with raffles, fortune tellers, games, and toys. Many boys and girls are in costumes. Others march in their school uniforms as part of the festive parade. Our Lady of Guadalupe corn cakes are a must at the yearly fiesta in the cathedral of Our Lady of Guadalupe as well. And, of course, there are flowers everywhere to add to the festive atmosphere.

No fiesta would be complete without lots of food! Fruits and vegetables, sticks of sugar cane, and gorditas (plump tortillas) are among some of the foods offered at Our Lady of Guadalupe fiestas. Some market stalls sell pupusas. Pupusas are thick tortillas (¾") filled with cheese or bacon. In addition, bakers start their doughs at 3-4 a.m., and hungry breakfasters arrive to smell, buy, and eat these wonderful works of art. The breads, rolls, and cakes are almost the same all over the country and keep popping out of ovens until the late afternoon.

Note: These activities involve subjects surrounding religious celebrations. Some children may be sensitive to this issue. Send a note home to parents or guardians before beginning this section. If, in your judgment, the activities in this lesson may be disturbing to children or parents, you might choose not to use them.

DAY OF OUR LADY OF GUADALUPE FIESTA

Sponsor a Day of Our Lady of Guadalupe fiesta in your classroom. The following ideas will help make this special holiday celebration come alive for the children.

CLASSROOM ENRICHMENT ACTIVITIES

MARBLES

Games are a part of most fiestas in Mexico and Central America. Introduce a Mexican and Central American version of the game of marbles to the children. Cut holes of varying sizes and shapes in one side of a shoebox. Write numbers above each hole according to its size—the highest number above the smallest hole, the lowest number above the largest hole, and so on.

Set the box in a designated spot. Position the players in a row about six feet from the box. Give each player a bag of marbles. Invite the children to take turns trying to shoot their marbles into the holes. If the marbles fail to go in any of the holes, the owners pick them up and keep them. However, if a player successfully shoots a marble into one of the holes, the player sitting to the right of that player must pay the successful player in marbles according to the number written above the hole. The player with the most marbles left when a player goes out of the game is the winner!

MARKETPLACE

Marketplaces are alive with lots of people during fiesta times. Help the children set up an Our Lady of Guadalupe marketplace in the classroom (or outside, if the weather permits). Invite parents and other classes to attend the market. Suggest that children bring old toys, pottery, and candles from home to sell at the market. Decorate the marketplace with lots of paper flowers (see pages 95-98). Some children may wish to set up stalls to sell the traditional Our Lady of Guadalupe corn cakes and pupusas wrapped in colorful tissue paper (see pages 152 and 160). Cut, bundled, and tied sugar-cane sticks are popular and fun for children to enjoy as well. Play some Mexican fiesta music to add a finishing touch to this festive occasion! (See the bibliography provided on pages 239-240.) ¡Olé!

PAPER FLOWERS

Flowers add color to a fiesta and help create a light-hearted atmosphere. All sizes, shapes, and colors of flowers appear everywhere during Mexican and Central American celebrations. Show the children how to make paper flowers (see pages 95-98) and then turn the children loose making flowers to decorate the classroom for their fiesta!

PAPIER-MÂCHÉ FRUITS AND VEGETABLES

People all over Mexico and Central America bring their fruits and vegetables to marketplaces to sell. Help the children make papier-mâché fruits and vegetables to "sell" in a classroom marketplace (see page 116). These are formed using real fruit. You might send letters home to parents requesting that they send some fruits and vegetables to school for this project.

STICK HORSES

Toys are a tradition at most Mexican and Central American fiestas. The children will enjoy making stick horses to "ride" in their Day of Our Lady of Guadalupe celebration parade (see pages 137-138). Point out that horses were brought to Mexico and Central America by the Europeans. There were no horses before the European discovery of the Americas.

CORN CAKES

Corn cakes are a tradition in the cathedral of Our Lady of Guadalupe in Mexico City. These cakes are wrapped in colored tissue paper and tied with ribbon for fun. Invite the children to make corn cakes to serve during the class Day of Our Lady of Guadalupe fiesta or to sell at the class market (see page 152).

SPOON BREAD

Spoon bread is fun to eat for Our Lady of Guadalupe celebrations. Invite the children to help make spoon bread for the class fiesta (see page 163). Ask the children how this bread probably got its name!

PUPUSAS

In the 16th century, Honduras and El Salvador were a part of Mexico. The Our Lady of Guadalupe festival is still celebrated in these countries as a result of that union. Pupusas, a dish from Honduras and El Salvador, is a traditional food served for Our Lady of Guadalupe celebrations. Invite the children to help make pupusas for the class fiesta (see page 160).

CANCIÓN DE CUNA (CRADLE SONG)

One of the beautiful parts of Mexican and Central American fiestas is the tradition of including children in the celebrations. Games are played and toys are made and given to children as special gifts. The children develop a cultural pride and sense of who they are. Teach the children the song *Canción de Cuna* (see pages 207-208).

GLOBAL AWARENESS

The following questions will help the children build bridges of understanding between Mexican and Central American cultures and their own cultures.

1. The people of Mexico and Central America erected a shrine to help them remember the vision of Our Lady of Guadalupe. In the United States, we have also erected shrines or monuments in the memory of important events or people. What are some of these shrines or monuments? Why were they erected?
2. The image of Mary on the blue tilma is found on churches, buses, canned goods, and in other places in Mexico. What images are found printed on items in the United States?
3. If you could create a holiday for some special event in your life, what would it be? How might the holiday be celebrated?

POSADA PROCESSION DAY

December 16

The Posada Procession is held on December 16, the day chosen in Mexico and Central America to begin the festivities for the Christmas celebration. The procession is held for eight nights. Traditionally, friends gather together in small groups. They carry a nacimiento (manger scene) as they go caroling from house to house looking for a place to stay. Children often pull a nacimiento in their wagons. By prearrangement, the carolers are turned down at many homes until they are finally invited into a designated home for the fiesta. Hosts serve the carolers cookies and punch.

Piñatas are traditional at Christmas time in Mexican and Central American cultures. A piñata is suspended from a beam or long pole. A rope is attached so that the piñata may be moved up and down. A child is blindfolded, given a bat or stick, and then turned around several times. Everyone sings "Dále! Dále! Dále!" ("Dále!" means "Hit it!" in Spanish) as the child tries to hit the piñata with the stick. The person holding the rope tries to keep the piñata out of the child's reach. All the children are given chances to hit the piñata until it breaks open. Then all the children are invited to scramble for the goodies that spill out!

When the Spanish conquerors were colonizing Mexico, they discovered a similar holiday celebrated by the Aztecs on December 17. The Spanish Christmas festivities blended some of the Aztec traditions with its own to fill the void left by the removal of that Aztec holiday.

POSADA PROCESSION DAY FIESTA

Sponsor a Posada Procession Day fiesta in your classroom. The following ideas will help make this special holiday celebration come alive for the children.

CLASSROOM ENRICHMENT ACTIVITIES

MIXING THE OLD AND NEW

Some Mexican and Central American pictures show women wearing the headdress of the Tehuana, women from Tehuantepec. This type of headdress supposedly originated when a ship was wrecked off a coast and a box of baby dresses washed ashore. The Tehuana, having never seen baby dresses before, weren't sure how they might be worn, so they used the dresses for headdresses. They unknowingly set a style that is still in vogue in parts of Mexico and Central America today!

Share this story with the children and then challenge them to create new uses for objects in the classroom. Encourage the children to illustrate their ideas as well.

POSADA SCAVENGER HUNT

Sponsor a scavenger hunt to gather items for the class Posada Procession Day fiesta (or to fill a class piñata—see pages 124-125). Help the children make a list of items that might be put in the piñata. Then, each day for eight days, encourage small groups of children to scavenge their neighborhoods (under adult supervision) or other classrooms seeking the items on the list.

PIÑATAS

Share some of the background information about the Posada Procession Day with the children. Ask the children if they have ever broken open a piñata. Suggest that the children bring to school items that they might use to fill a piñata. Then help the children make a class piñata (see pages 124-125). For gifts, invite the children to make individual piñata creatures using toilet-paper rolls with oranges for the heads. Fill the individual piñatas with the children's goodies and hang them in the classroom. Break open the class piñata on the last day of school before winter vacation. Invite the children to take their individual piñatas home to give as gifts or to use as part of their families' traditional festivities.

ENSALADA DE NOCHEBUENA (CHRISTMAS EVE SALAD)

Ask the children if their families serve special foods for particular holidays. Discuss how traditions are established and handed down from family to family and from one culture to another. Invite the children to share interesting stories about the traditions behind the serving of holiday foods in their families. Explain that Ensalada de Nochebuena is a traditional Mexican and Central American salad served on Christmas Eve. Help the children make the salad (see page 153). Then ask the children to suggest reasons why this salad probably became a tradition. Give each child a copy of the recipe. Suggest that children take the recipe home to share with members of their families. Maybe they will want to make this salad a part of their family holiday traditions, too.

POLVORONES (MEXICAN WEDDING CAKES)

Polvorones are wonderful fiesta cookies to serve for Posada Procession Day fiesta. Explain that polvo means "dust" in Spanish. Invite the children to help make Polvorones (see page 159). Then ask the children to predict why the Spaniards probably named these cookies as they did.

NIÑO QUERIDO (DEAREST CHILD)

Teach the children the song *Niño Querido* (see pages 213-214).

PARA QUEBRAR LA PIÑATA (BREAKING THE PIÑATA)

Games are a fun part of every celebration. The breaking of a piñata is an especially delightful Mexican and Central American game. Young and old alike enjoy this game so much that they play it at almost every fiesta! Teach the children the song *Para Quebrar la Piñata* to sing as they break open a class piñata (see pages 220-223).

GLOBAL AWARENESS

The following questions will help the children build bridges of understanding between Mexican and Central American cultures and their own cultures.

1. Which holiday in the United States is similar to the Mexican and Central American celebration of the Posada Procession Day? How are the celebrations alike? How are they different?
2. What part of the Posada Day celebration is familiar to you?
3. What part of the Posada Procession Day fiesta did you enjoy the most? Why?

DAY OF THE THREE KINGS

January 6

In Mexico and Central America, the celebration of Christmas begins on December 16, but young children receive gifts on January 6, the Day of the Three Kings (El Dia de los Tres Reyes).

On January 5, children write letters to the wise men (Magi) and put them in their shoes. Nacimientos (nativity scenes) are set out the evening of January 5 and the Magi place the children's gifts near the nacimientos. Children leave a bundle of hay or a pot of water for the Kings' camels.

A traditional big bread (Rosca de los Reyes) is baked and cut into small pieces and enjoyed by all the family. The bread has a small doll baked inside. The person who finds the doll in his or her bread piece is blessed with good luck and gives a party for the gathered guests on Candlemas Day, February 2, the day Mexicans and Central Americans bless the seeds for a bountiful harvest (see page 48).

Mexican and Central Americans have been far ahead of North Americans in their love of making and giving toy miniatures to children as gifts. Miniatures are made for the Day of the Three Kings from clay or chicle. Chicle comes from the Sapodilla tree.

The Day of the Three Kings is as much a part of Central American culture as Thanksgiving is in the United States.

DAY OF THE THREE KINGS FIESTA

Sponsor a Day of the Three Kings fiesta in your classroom. The following ideas will help make this special holiday celebration come alive for the children.

CLASSROOM ENRICHMENT ACTIVITIES

CHANTS AND POEMS

Share information about the Day of the Three Kings celebration in Mexico and Central America and then invite the children to write short poems or chants about their impressions of this fiesta. Help the children write one or more poems together as a class first. Then divide the class into small cooperative-learning groups. Encourage the children to write poems or chants about other interesting facts they know about Mexico and Central America as well. Share the finished poems and chants together in class as part of the Day of the Three Kings festivities.

BALLOONS

Mix 1 tablespoon kitchen cleanser per cup of tempera paint and invite the children to use the mixture to paint clowns, explorers, animals, or other images on inflated balloons. Use the balloons to decorate the classroom.

CHICLE-ART TOY MINIATURES

Chicle is a latex liquid that comes from Sapodilla trees. A "v" is cut in the bark of the tree and the liquid oozes out. This is what gum is made from.

To make gum, the latex sap is boiled and kneaded to remove any excess liquid. Vegetable colors are put in the whitish substance to make pretty colors. There are chicle manufacturing companies in the Yucatan and Guatemala. The latex sap is combined with spices and then packaged and distributed all over the world. Chicle sculpture started in the lands of the Maya in the Yucatan and Guatemala.

Invite the children to chew gum of different colors. When the gum is soft and pliable, it may be pulled like taffy and rolled, woven, and shaped into miniature sculptures. The classic miniature in Mexico and Central America is that of children riding atop a crocodile. Other popular miniatures are little burros and teeny figures.

Have the children work on wax paper, since the gum will be sticky! **Caution the children to only handle their own gum.** Have the children wash their hands when they are finished sculpting! Invite the children to take their miniatures home.

FROG PIÑATA

No Mexican and Central American celebration would be complete without games or a piñata. Piñatas may be made in any shape. Just for fun, challenge the children to help create a class frog piñata (see pages 126-128).

DONKEY

All over Mexico and Central America, baker's clay is used to make miniatures. Clay is plentiful and easy to mold into the kinds of toys typically seen all over Mexico and Central America. Baker's clay pieces are heavy and fragile.

Invite the children to make clay miniatures of a donkey (see page 83). The miniatures may be adorned with yarn, cloth, paint, or buttons and bows. White glue will hold almost anything on a flat painted surface before it is shellacked. Display the finished miniatures in the classroom as part of a Day of the Three Kings display.

PAPIER-MÂCHÉ MASKS

Masks from Mexico and Central America combine the best of two cultures—Native American vigor and Spanish grace. Encourage the children to be creative and design joyous masks in brilliant colors (see pages 117-119). Invite the children to wear their finished masks in a Day of the Three Kings parade. After the parade, pin the masks on a bulletin board. The masks will make a colorful display and remind the children of their fun Day of the Three Kings fiesta!

TREE OF LIFE

In Mexico, clay is used to make a tree of life. The tree represents a new beginning. It is decorated with flower and animal designs.

Make a tree of life or a tree of life wall hanging together with your class (see pages 139-142). One group might make the base, while other groups of children make figurines or blossoms. There are many types of Mexican scenes portrayed on a tree of life. A Puebla tree of life is shown on cacti adorned with happy dog figures.

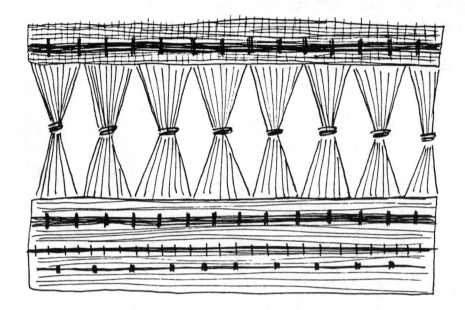

The people of Mexico and Central America make a variety of lovely weavings. Each piece is an original—no two serapes (woolen wraps) are the same! Weavers create their own unique designs and decide which colors of yarn to use. Invite the children to make simple looms on which they might weave original designs (see pages 143-144). Suggest that children pin their finished weavings on their shirts to add a Mexican and Central American flavor to their clothing. Display the weavings in the classroom for several days. Encourage the children to look for the originality of each design.

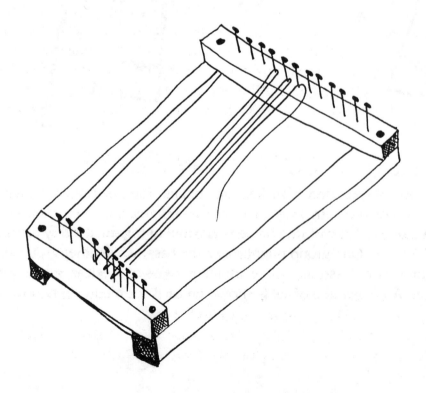

ROSCA DE LOS REYES (KINGS' BREAD)

In Mexico and Central America, seasons and holidays are reflected in the shapes the loaves of bread are made. For the Day of the Three Kings, bread is shaped like a king's crown. Candied fruits and nuts placed into the crown's top sparkle like jewels.

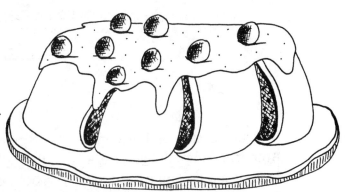

Help the children make Rosca de los Reyes (see page 149). Bake a little porcelain doll or a lima bean in the bread as a surprise. Caution children to be careful as they eat their pieces. Invite the class to decide what the child who receives the piece of bread with a doll or lima bean in it must do (bring treats for the class, clean a pet cage for a week, and so on). Have fun!

EL COQUÍ (THE CROAKER)

Many Mexican and Central American celebrations involve animals. Animal figures are used to decorate a tree of life and as subjects for making toy miniatures. Teach the children the song *El Coquí* (see pages 224-227). Have the children sing the song as they take turns trying to break open a frog piñata (see pages 126-128).

MARIMBA

Music is an important part of the Day of the Three Kings fiestas. Play a tape or record of some Mexican and Central American music. Encourage the children to listen carefully to the sounds they hear (guitars, marimbas, maracas, and other percussion instruments). Discuss how the music makes them feel. Show the children how to make simple marimbas using pop bottles (see page 171). Then invite children to play their marimbas along with the Mexican and Central American music!

GLOBAL AWARENESS

The following questions will help the children build bridges of understanding between Mexican and Central American cultures and their own cultures.

1. Santa Claus is found in one form or another in almost every culture of the world. (Santa Claus is relatively new to most Mexican and Central American children. He is found only in the larger cities.) What parts of the Mexican and Central American Day of the Three Kings celebration compares to Santa Claus and Christmas customs in the United States?

2. Some Mexicans and Central Americans make valuable porcelain-like figures with chicle (gum). What else might you use chicle for?

BLESSING OF THE ANIMALS

January 17

The Blessing of the Animals is a popular fiesta throughout Mexico and Central America. Animals are revered and thought by some to have mystical powers. This fiesta is a blending of attitudes from both early Native American civilizations and the European influences.

On January 17, people decorate their chickens, ducks, pigs, oxen, dogs, and other animals with flowers and ribbons and take them to the church to be blessed by a religious leader.

In many villages, animal parades take place as well. Some animals are adorned with flowers, many are draped with crepe-paper streamers, and a few are painted with food coloring. You might even see a little pig with brightly painted nail polish!

Colorful murals are painted in Mexico as part of the Blessing of the Animals fiesta. The murals are usually full of animal paintings. Some are rural scenes, others are of villages, activities at school, or maybe parades. Sometimes the murals are small elegant paintings of an animal, such as a deer or chicken.

BLESSING OF THE ANIMALS FIESTA

Sponsor a Blessing of the Animals fiesta in your classroom. The following ideas will help make this special holiday celebration come alive for the children.

CLASSROOM ENRICHMENT ACTIVITIES

ANIMAL PARADE

Share some of the background information about the Blessing of the Animals fiesta with the children. Encourage the children to brainstorm ways they might dress up various animals.

Invite the children to dress up their pets and bring them to school on a designated Blessing of the Animals Day for an animal parade. Children may bring stuffed animals if they wish as well. Invite parents and other classes to attend the parade.

AMATE-PAPER ANIMAL FUN

Amate-paper art is a special Mexican folk craft. Plants and animals provide the basic design elements. Ask the children if they have some Mexican amate paper at home that they might bring to school to share. Amate paper is a favorite item to buy at Mexican markets.

Show the children how to make amate paper in bright colors (see page 80). Suggest that children paint pictures of their favorite animals or pets on the paper using colored chalk and sugar water, or tempera paint mixed with canned milk or liquid starch. Then encourage the children to write stories about their illustrations.

MIGAJON ANIMALS

Migajon is a bread-based modeling clay. This craft is found all over Mexico and Central America. Miniature animals are popular objects to make from migajon. Help the children make a list of the animals they might make from migajon. Encourage them to think of unusual animals as well as common animals. Then turn the children's imaginations loose! Invite children to make several animals from migajon (see page 103) to contribute to a classroom "Blessing of the Animals Zoo."

HAIRY CHIA ARMADILLO

Ask the children if they have ever seen an armadillo. Explain that armadillos are common animals in Mexico and Central America. They like warm climates. Ask the children to discuss how armadillos adapt well to warm climates. Invite the children to make some fun Hairy Chia Armadillos (see pages 100-101).

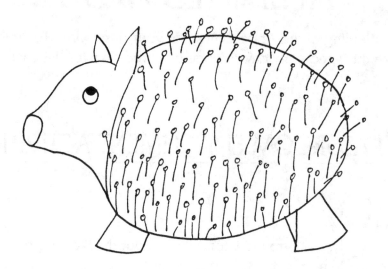

PIGGY BANK

Ask the children if they have piggy banks at home. Encourage the children to suggest reasons why coin banks are often shaped like pigs. Brainstorm a list of other animals that might make good banks as well. Then invite the children to make piggy banks or other animal banks (see pages 122-123). Suggest that children write stories about how their pigs feel about being used as banks, as well as other feelings pigs might have about their reputations.

CHICKEN TOSTADAS

Six thousand years ago, corn was first grown by the people of Mexico and Central America. Before long, these early farmers discovered that they could grind the kernels of corn with a stone mortar or pestle to make cornmeal. By mixing the cornmeal with water, they prepared a dough that could be made into very thin pancakes. They tossed the pancakes onto rocks placed in a fire and the tortilla was born. Today, tortillas are eaten everywhere in Mexico with almost every meal! They are a basis for many popular Mexican foods, such as tostadas. Invite the children to make Chicken Tostadas (see page 151) to celebrate the past, present, and future!

MARACA BANK

Mexican and Central American fiestas are loud and boisterous! Give small groups of children two paper cups, some coins, tape, paper scraps, glue, and a variety of other scrap materials. Challenge the children in each group to make an animal noisemaker using the provided materials. Invite the children to share their finished noisemakers with the class. Discuss the sounds each noisemaker makes. Encourage the children to experiment adding and subtracting coins from the cups and comparing the sounds made when the noisemakers are shaken.

After the class Blessing of the Animals fiesta, invite the children to take their maracas home, cut slits in the top, and use the maracas for piggy (or other animal) banks!

ANIMAL MUSIC REVUE

Help the children brainstorm a list of songs about animals (*Old MacDonald Had a Farm, Mary Had a Little Lamb, Rubber Ducky,* and so on). Invite the children to sing the songs they name as well. Then teach the children the following Mexican and Central American songs about animals. Encourage individuals or small groups of children to write their own verses for these songs. The children will have a great time writing original lyrics—the more outrageous the lyrics, the more fun. Suggest that children shake maracas in time to the songs as other individuals or groups of children perform their original songs for the class.

A Mambrú Chato (Pugnosed Mambrú), pages 193-196

Arre, Caballito (Get Along, My Pony), pages 228-231

El Coyotillo (Little Coyote), pages 185-190

GLOBAL AWARENESS

The following questions will help children build bridges of understanding between Mexican and Central American cultures and their own cultures.

1. Animals are the focus of the Blessing of the Animals fiesta. What North American holidays feature animals?
2. Mexican and Central Americans bless animals on Blessing of the Animals fiesta to show their love and respect for animals. In what ways are animals protected and cared for in the United States?
3. Sometimes Mexican and Central Americans paint the toenails of animals to decorate them for the Blessing of the Animals parade. What animals might be in a parade in your area? How might you dress them?

CANDLEMAS

February 2

February 2 is Candlemas Day all over Mexico and Central America, the day of the blessing of the seeds or crops. Today, there are many kinds of Mexican and Central American fiestas held in conjunction with Candlemas. In the country, elaborate festivals include lit candles and food. Traditionally, amate-paper witches are made and placed in fields and gardens to protect the crops. These dolls are called *brujas*. White brujas are believed to bring good spirits, while brown brujas are believed to ward off evil spirits. The brujas are stacked on the ground by the crops. In the Otomi culture of San Pablito, the state of Puebla, there are as many different doll patterns as there are fruits and vegetables to protect.

CANDLEMAS FIESTA

Sponsor a Candlemas fiesta in your classroom. The following ideas will help make this special holiday celebration come alive for the children.

CLASSROOM ENRICHMENT ACTIVITIES

CLASSROOM GARDEN

Bring to school a variety of vegetables. Point out that corn and black beans are commonly found in Mexico and Central America. Discuss the growing conditions needed to raise corn and beans.

Invite the children to bring vegetable seeds to school, such as peppers, corn, parsley, onions, garlic, and other crops that might later be used in classroom cooking. Help the children plant the seeds in individual pots or in a classroom patio garden. Make a growing chart for the crops you plant.

INVITATIONS

Ask the children who they might invite to their Candlemas fiesta. Suggest that children make invitations to send to the invited guests. Have the children draw and cut out brown and white paper witches (see page 81). Mount the brown paper witches on folded sheets of white construction paper and the white witches on folded sheets of brown construction paper. Bright-colored tissue paper also makes lovely witches.

HAIRY CHIA ARMADILLO

Show the children a picture of an armadillo. Point out that armadillos live in warm areas of the Americas. Encourage the children to describe the armadillo. Invite the children to make a fun armadillo planter for chia seeds (see pages 100-101).

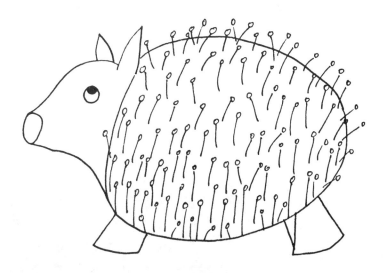

MURAL

Hang a long sheet of butcher paper along a classroom wall. Invite the children to paint a mural scene showing the planting and harvesting of corn, flower seeds, and other crops (see page 107).

PAPER FLOWERS

Discuss the uses of flowers in the United States. How do flowers make people feel? Is there a connection between how flowers make people feel and the occasions when flowers are sent to people? Flowers are a part of every Mexican and Central American fiesta because they are plentiful and because of the feelings and party atmosphere they create.

Help the children make a variety of paper flowers to decorate the classroom (see pages 95-98). Flowers are found all over Mexico and Central America during fiesta time. In Nicaragua, people even make flowers from cornhusks. If possible, have the children bring real flowers to school for this fiesta, too. Perhaps a local florist will contribute. Fill the classroom with flowers!

GUACAMOLE (AVOCADO SAUCE)

Show the children an avocado. Ask them if they know what is inside. Carefully peel the avocado and then cut it in half to expose the seed. Explain that avocados are used to make sauces for chips or to pour over many Mexican dishes. The seed may be planted as well! Help the children make guacamole (see page 155). Use the guacamole to make a taco platter (see page 164). Invite the children to plant the avocado seeds in the classroom garden (see page 49).

TACO PLATTER

Corn is one of the most frequent crops raised in Mexico and Central America. Many Mexican foods evolved from corn. Help the children brainstorm a list of foods their families eat that come from corn. Discuss the children's favorite ways of eating corn. Explain that the tortilla was invented in Mexico by the Native Americans that lived there long ago. Native American corn comes in many colors. The color of corn used to make tortilla flour determines the color of the tortillas. In the mid-1900s and before, tortillas were made fresh daily in almost every household. Today they are usually mass-produced.

Help the children make and assemble a taco platter, a delicious dip to serve with tortilla chips (see page 164).

MARACAS

In Mexico and Central America, dried gourds are used to make maracas. The seeds inside harden and make wonderful rattling sounds when the gourd is shaken. Help the children make maracas from dried gourds and other materials to shake in a class Candlemas parade (see pages 168-170).

GLOBAL AWARENESS

The following questions will help the children build bridges of understanding between Mexican and Central American cultures and their own cultures.

1. Candlemas has its roots in agriculture. Are there any celebrations in the United States that focus on the celebration of planting or harvest? If so, how are they celebrated?
2. How are the use of amate witches and the use of scarecrows similar?

 # CARNIVAL
February

Huge carnivals are held in Brazil, but delightful smaller ones are held all over Mexico and Central America. Part of the tradition of Carnival is wearing masks and colorful costumes and dancing in parades. Usually the first marchers are uniformed youngsters from schools. Carnival fiestas are held in homes, private clubs, or in public places, such as schools and even government buildings. Carnival occurs on Shrove Tuesday (the day before Ash Wednesday, the beginning of Lent), although the date is changeable because it is based on the lunar calendar. The Carnival celebration was introduced to Mexico and Central America by the Europeans.

CARNIVAL FIESTA

Sponsor a Carnival fiesta in your classroom. The following ideas will help make this special holiday celebration come alive for the children.

CLASSROOM ENRICHMENT ACTIVITIES

INVITATIONS

Invite the children to decide on a guest list for their Carnival fiesta. Suggest that children make invitations by folding sheets of amate paper (see page 80) or construction paper in half and then decorating the covers with crispy flowers. These are made by cutting out flower shapes from colored tissue paper. Dabs of glue are dropped on the areas where flowers are to be placed and then the tissue-paper shapes are pressed on the glue. Help the children plan and write messages on the insides of the invitations once the glue has dried.

PARADE

Invite the children to wear brightly colored costumes and masks on a designated day for a Carnival parade. Lead the children in a parade around the school grounds. Arrange for other classes and invited guests to line the parade route!

BALLOONS

Balloons play an important role in Mexican and Central American fiestas. They are bright and pretty, whether filled with helium or air. Invite the children to paint carnival images (clown faces, pets, flowers, and so on) on inflated balloons, first with a coat of kitchen cleanser and then with tempera paint. If possible, rent a helium tank and fill the balloons with helium so the children may carry the balloons in their Carnival parade.

FILL-AND-SPILL EGGS

Fill-and-spill eggs add color and help to create a celebration spirit. Children will have fun making these eggs and then breaking them open over their friends' heads! Invite the children to make fill-and-spill eggs for their Carnival celebration (see page 94).

FEATHER MASKS

Feather masks are fun to make and wear. They give a classroom celebration a real Carnival atmosphere. Feather masks evolved from an old Aztec belief about a beloved god called Quetzalcóatl, the feathered serpent with the green mask. He was thought to be such a miracle worker that he made the corn grow to enormous sizes. The Aztecs thought they were safe as long as Quetzalcóatl was among them. Feather masks are seen everywhere in Mexico and Central America, but especially at Carnival time. Invite the children to make feather masks to wear in their Carnival parade (see pages 92-93).

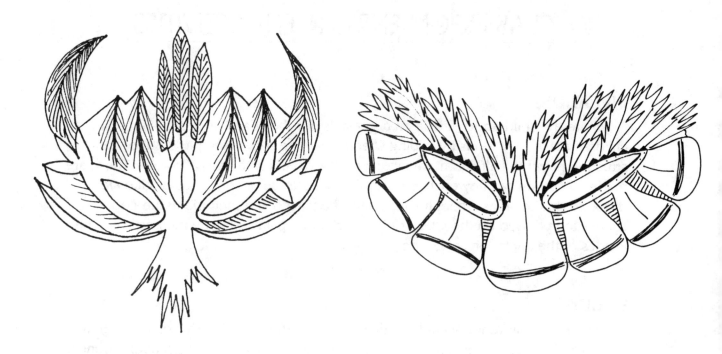

PAPER FLOWERS

Suggest that the children make a variety of decorations for the Carnival fiesta. Paper flowers are a favorite for Mexican and Central American celebrations. Paper flowers are made throughout Mexico, Central America, and most of South America. Encourage the children to think of some unique blooming ideas (see pages 95-98).

PAPER-PLATE MASKS

It's fun to be somebody else during Carnival and to wear fine masks and wonderful costumes. Sponsor a paper mask-making contest. Encourage the children to make masks from paper plates with a variety of paper scraps and other odds and ends. Use popsicle sticks or tongue depressors as handles for the masks. Suggest that children research and then make masks of famous people connected with the exploration and settlement of Mexico and Central America, or famous modern-day Mexican and Central Americans—Cortez, Montezuma, or Eva Peron, for example (younger children might make masks of important people in their lives). Invite the children to wear the finished masks in their Carnival parade.

GORDITAS (PLUMP TORTILLAS)

Carnival is celebrated on Shrove Tuesday, also known as Fat Tuesday. The name evolves from an old custom. People would clean their shelves of fat, eggs, and other foods forbidden during Lent and then use the banned foods to make pancakes, doughnuts, and other rich foods!

Shrove Tuesday is celebrated in schools all over Mexico and Central America. Special songs are played and sung by the children and holiday foods for the special day are shared. Help the children prepare gorditas to serve invited guests at their Carnival fiesta (see page 154).

CONGA AND SAMBA LINES

In Mexico and Central America, dance is one of the major forms of expression. Native Americans, Africans, and Spanish and Portuguese conquerors and settlers have all contributed to the variety and color apparent in Mexican and Central American dances. Carnival attracts thousands of costumed dancers annually. They dance the favorite and traditional rhythms of each country.

Ask the physical education teacher in your school to teach the Conga and Samba to the children. Then help the children form a line and perform these dances as part of their Carnival fiesta parade.

BALLOON MARACAS

Guitars, marimbas, and other Mexican and Central American instruments help set a fiesta mood. It's hard to sit still when Mexican and Central American music is playing. Play some lively Mexican and Central American music for the children (see the bibliography provided on pages 239-240). Discuss different ways that the children might respond to the music (tap their feet, snap their fingers, dance, clap their hands). Focus the children's attention on the percussion instruments. If possible, show the children a maraca. Invite them to experiment making different sounds. Ask the children what they think is probably inside the maraca. Then help the children make some balloon maracas to shake during their Carnival parade (see page 168).

GLOBAL AWARENESS

The following questions will help the children build bridges of understanding between Mexican and Central American cultures and their own cultures.

1. Carnival is celebrated with huge parades. People wear masks and other costumes while they dance. What North American holidays are celebrated in a similar manner?
2. We have carnivals in this country, too. What are carnivals like in the United States? How are they different from Carnival in Mexico and Central America?

♥×♥ ST. JOSEPH'S DAY ♥×♥

March 19

St. Joseph's Day is a big fiesta in Costa Rica. Each country in Central America has its own patron saint. A holiday is always celebrated in the saint's honor. The saint for Costa Rica is St. Joseph.

Early on, settlers came from Europe to Costa Rica, but the land wasn't very productive and few people survived there. It was only after its independence from Spain in 1821 and the subsequent civil war giving "freedom to Costa Rica" that Costa Rica as a country finally developed. Costa Rica's roots are Spanish, Mestizo, and, in a remote region, Indian.

In 1825, the government offered free Costa Rican land to coffee growers. Within twenty-five years, coffee produced from the new plantations was being exported to other parts of the world—transported to the coast in small ox carts. Replicas of these carts are made in different sizes using a variety of materials and different colors. In the country today, many people still use these beautifully decorated carts to carry their fruits and vegetables to the market.

Costa Rica's development is unique in Central America. The population of Costa Rica is about ninety percent Spanish. However, customs from both Spain and Italy are evident in its St. Joseph's Day celebration. The most beautiful art pieces are displayed on this day, especially portraits of St. Joseph.

Special breads are baked, Lenten foods are prepared, and gifts are exchanged. Visits to at least five homes for festive meals are traditional as well.

ST. JOSEPH'S DAY FIESTA

Sponsor a St. Joseph's Day fiesta in your classroom. The following ideas will help make this special holiday celebration come alive for the children.

CLASSROOM ENRICHMENT ACTIVITIES

CRAFT MARKETPLACE

Invite the children to make baskets, clay dolls, coil pots (see pages 84-87), and other items to sell in a class marketplace (see page 31).

WHERE IS COSTA RICA?

To encourage the children to learn more about the uniqueness of Costa Rica, sponsor an information hunt. Challenge the children to see who can find the most interesting facts about Costa Rica. Encourage the children to suggest categories. When each child has had an opportunity to find as much information as possible, divide the class into small groups to share their responses. Have the children decide as a group on one answer to each question listed here that they feel no other group will suggest. Then survey the groups for the results. Each group is awarded a point for each answer they give that no other group suggests.

What is the most unusual fact you found?

What is the most interesting fact you found?

Name one way Costa Rica is like other Mexican and Central American countries.

Name two ways Costa Rica is different from other Mexican and Central American countries.

BASKETS

Native markets in Costa Rica carry a wide selection of handmade objects. Baskets are a favorite, and in some cases, a necessity for the native Costa Ricans. Baskets are used to carry items from place to place, as is done in other countries of the world as well. Invite the children to make baskets to display in the classroom for a St. Joseph's Day celebration (see page 84). Then invite the children to take the baskets home to use as containers for their special possessions.

MURAL

Homes in cities and in the country alike in Costa Rica are very colorful, painted in pinks, greens, and blues. Show the children some pictures of Costa Rican homes. Then hang a long sheet of butcher paper along one wall. Invite the children to paint scenes of a Costa Rican village (or of their own homes) using pink, green, and blue tempera paint (see page 107).

OX CART

Costa Ricans use beautifully decorated ox carts to carry their fruits and vegetables to market. Their love of color is evident in the dazzling designs painstakingly painted on these carts. Each design is unique, and, just like a coat of arms, is passed on from generation to generation. Invite the children to make replicas of these beautiful ox carts (see page 110). Encourage each child to create a unique design to paint on his or her cart.

MEXICAN BANANA BAKE

Costa Rica is an agricultural country. Bananas are the second most important export in Costa Rica. Bananas are grown primarily along the coastal regions. Show the children a plantain. Plantains are little green bananas, curved at one end, with a thick skin. Sometimes they are called *bread bananas.* They are available in most grocery stores in the United States. If they are not available in your area, large bananas may be substituted. Invite the children to make Mexican Banana Bake, a delicious holiday treat to serve for their St. Joseph's Day fiesta (see page 157).

MARIMBA

Costa Rican folk music is most often played on the guitar and the marimba. Many of the marimbas are so large that several musicians may play them at one time! Help the children make replicas of a marimba to play in the classroom for their St. Joseph's Day fiesta (see page 171).

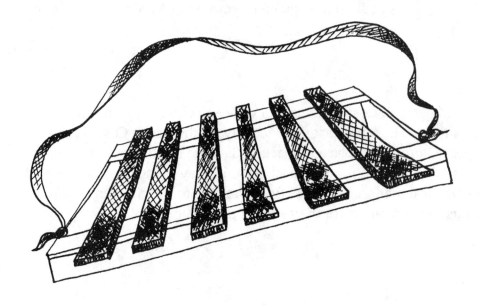

GLOBAL AWARENESS

The following questions will help the children build bridges of understanding between Mexican and Central American cultures and their own cultures.

1. Costa Rica's population is more than ninety percent Spanish. The St. Joseph's Day celebration has much evidence of Spanish influence with its food and drink. How does this compare to St. Patrick's Day celebrations in the United States?

2. The banana is a fruit that is native to Costa Rica. It is served for special holidays. What foods native to the area in which you live are commonly served for holiday celebrations?

3. List ways that the area in which you live is like Costa Rica. What one unique way is the area in which you live different from Costa Rica?

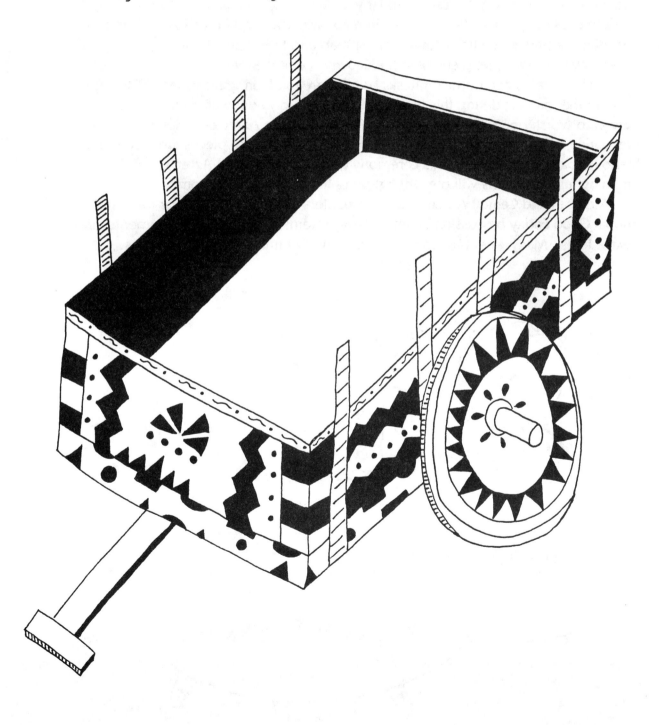

# EASTER

March/April

Easter in Mexico and Central America is in late March or early April. This celebration usually includes Palm Sunday, a celebration that has a permanent place in the Mexican and Central American calendar year.

On the Friday before Palm Sunday in many Mexican and Central American towns or cities, carpets made from flowers are spread and little pots of flowers pop up all over town. Flowers are plentiful in Mexico and Central America.

Palm pieces made from cornhusks or raffia are made in great variety. They are sold in the markets during this time of the year, used to decorate churches, and given to worshippers on Palm Sunday. There are some Aztec ceremonies that have remained in use during this time of the year. After the palm pieces are made, the leftover palms are burned. This ceremony comes from the old Aztec belief that burning leftover palms will prevent lightning from striking their homes.

Mexican and Central Americans make papier-mâché masks to wear for a traditional Good Friday procession. People carry lanterns, play musical instruments, and wave flags. Many wear traditional Mexican and Central American costumes.

EASTER FIESTA

Sponsor an Easter fiesta in your classroom. The following ideas will help make this special holiday celebration come alive for the children.

CLASSROOM ENRICHMENT ACTIVITIES

BASKETS

Many items found and used in Mexican and Central American homes can be traced back to Pre-Columbian days. For example, handwoven baskets are used all over Mexico and Central America. Show the children how to weave baskets from palm leaves or raffia (see page 84). Use the baskets in the classroom as part of a Mexican and Central American Easter display. Then invite the children to take their baskets home to give as gifts or to use as Easter baskets if this holiday is observed in their homes.

FILL-AND-SPILL EGGS

In the evening, after all the Easter parades and festivities are over, Mexicans and Central Americans meet in central plazas to enjoy band concerts. The retreta is a Spanish tradition that takes place on the plaza as well. Boys walk together around the plaza in one direction, while girls walk in the other. As they pass, the boys break open colored eggs filled with perfume or confetti and sprinkle the contents over the girls' heads. This encourages the girls to notice the boys and perhaps recognize the boys later when they meet again!

Help the children make fill-and-spill eggs to break open and sprinkle on the children who are invited to watch your Easter procession (see page 94).

FLOWER MATS

Flowers are plentiful in Mexico and Central America. They are found everywhere—in marketplaces, homes, restaurants, and even on the floor as mats! Flower mats are a delightful way to welcome the Easter celebration or for decoration throughout the year. Help the children weave strips of palm leaves (cornhusks, raffia, or even strips of light cardboard may be substituted) to make small mats (10" x 12"). Then paper flowers (or real flowers if possible—ask your local florist for a donation) may be glued on the mats for decoration. If real flowers are used, the children may carefully weave the stems of the flowers between the palm strips. Use these mats as placemats, or line up all of the children's mats on the floor and sew them together along the sides to make a large floor mat.

FROG PIÑATA

Piñatas are popular at most fiestas. Help the children make a frog piñata to represent the beginning of spring (see pages 126-128). Fill the piñata with tangerines, peanuts, sugar cane, and other Mexican and Central American goodies. Break the piñata open during your Easter fiesta.

LOCAL COLOR

Stitchery, applique, and weaving are popular all over Mexico and Central America. The weavings are always colorful and unique. The weavers in each country have their own characteristic designs. Early Maya and Aztec made their own dyes for yarn from the natural vegetation that grew in their areas. Invite the children to make some natural dyes from the weeds, grasses, berries, blossoms, and other colorful plants found in the area where they live (see page 102). Use the mixtures to dye fill-and-spill eggs (see page 94) or yarn for weaving projects (see page 143-144).

MEXICAN LANTERNS

Mexican lanterns are fun to make and carry in a classroom Easter parade. These are easily made by folding colorful sheets of construction paper in half the long way and then making cuts every ½" along the fold to within 1" of the opposite side. Unfold the cut papers and form them into lantern shapes by taping the top and bottom sides of the papers together. Encourage the children to take their lanterns home after the Easter fiesta at school is over.

PALM PIECES

Traditionally, Mexicans and Central Americans carry palm pieces in their Palm Sunday processions. Palm leaves are woven together by hand to create imaginative designs. Invite the children to weave palm leaves together, or strips of palm leaves, to create original designs (see page 111). If palm leaves are not available, cornhusks or raffia may be substituted. Encourage the children to carry their palm pieces in their Easter procession.

PAPIER-MÂCHÉ MASKS

Easter was brought to Mexico and Central America by the Spanish and other conquerors. Encourage the children to research some of the conquistadores of Mexico and Central America. Then invite the children to make papier-mâché masks (see pages 117-119) of some of these conquerors to wear for an Easter procession. After the procession, display the masks on a bulletin board entitled "Mexican and Central American Easter Parade."

SOPA SECA DE TORTILLA (TORTILLA CASSEROLE)

Tortillas are a staple food of Mexico and Central America. Sometimes tortillas are eaten three times a day! Point out similarities between tortillas and bread eaten in the United States and other countries. Although tortillas can be prepared in a variety of ways, Sopa Seca de Tortillas (see page 162) is a particularly delicious treat. Sopa means "soup," but don't let this fool you—sopa is a dry soup! The children will have fun making dry soup to serve guests at their Easter fiesta.

EL COQUÍ (THE CROAKER)

Easter usually represents the beginning of spring. Help the children make a list of some of the signs of spring. Ask the children to name some animals that hibernate and then wake up in the spring. Explain that frogs are hibernating creatures. Teach the children the song *El Coquí* (see pages 224-227) to sing as they try to break open a frog piñata (see pages 126-128).

MARIMBA

Music has been a part of the history of Mexico and Central America from Pre-Columbian times. The most sophisticated instrument designed by the early Maya and Aztec was the marimba, a form of the xylophone. Help the children make a modern-day version of the Pre-Columbian marimba using pop bottles (see page 171). Then invite the children to experiment playing different tunes on their marimbas.

GLOBAL AWARENESS

The following questions will help the children build bridges of understanding between Mexican and Central American cultures and their own cultures.

1. How is the Mexican and Central American celebration of Easter similar to Easter celebrations in the United States?
2. Why do you think flowers are such a special part of Mexican and Central American Easter celebrations? In what holidays in the United States do flowers play an important role?

 PAN-AMERICAN DAY

April 14

Since 1931, Pan-American Day has been observed in the United States and other republics of the Organization of American States. Many schools plan entertainment on April 14 that feature and promote the customs of Mexican and Central American nations.

The countries of Mexico and Central America are close neighbors to the United States. Simon Bolivar, a great South American leader, originated the idea of American unity. The first Treaty of Union was signed at the Congress of Panama in 1826. The first International Conference of American States, held in Washington D. C. in 1890, created the International Union of American Republics. All Mexican and Central American countries, with the exception of Santo Domingo, were present. The present organization, the Organization of American States (OAS), is an outgrowth of that union.

The Pan-American Union promotes goodwill and cooperation among the nations of the Western Hemisphere. The union pledges three main goals:

1. Mutual Defense. Many Mexican and Central American countries are small and vulnerable to attack. The nations promised to defend one another if attacked by unfriendly forces.

2. Peaceful Settlements. Disputing countries are encouraged to bring their conflicts to the OAS for negotiating settlements. Fighting is discouraged.

3. Human Rights. There has been an on-going concern to improve living conditions in Mexico and Central America. In 1961, President John F. Kennedy proposed the Alliance for Progress. His intent for this alliance was to improve housing, schools, highways, and other community concerns of Mexican and Central American countries.

An outgrowth of the Pan-American alliance is the Pan-American Games. These games were organized to encourage friendships among nations of the Western Hemisphere and to give amateur athletes experience in international competition. The games are held every four years in the year prior to the Olympic Games. The first Pan-American Games were held in Buenos Aires in 1951.

In 1936, the United States and the Mexican and Central American republics signed an agreement to build the Pan-American Highway. The Pan-American Highway is not one road, but a system of roads nearly 17,000 miles long. It is one of the world's great international highways bridging North and South America—crossing rivers and mountains, jungles and deserts. Travelers may stop along the way and visit sights of the major civilizations—Aztec, Maya, and Inca. They may also see towns in transition, from colonial to modern. The Pan-American Highway is important because it is a lifeline of commerce and friendship in the Americas.

PAN-AMERICAN DAY FIESTA

Sponsor a Pan-American Day fiesta in your classroom. The following ideas will help make this special holiday celebration come alive for the children.

CLASSROOM ENRICHMENT ACTIVITIES

PAN-AMERICAN BULLETIN BOARD

Designate a bulletin board in your classroom where children may post magazine and newspaper articles and other items related to Pan-American Day. Suggest that children also make drawings and cut out magazine pictures depicting goodwill among nations.

PAN-AMERICAN FAIR

Invite the children to share items from Mexican and Central American countries, such as baskets, bowls, hats, serapes, other special costumes, weavings, and so on. Display these items in an area in your classroom for several days for the children to enjoy. Encourage the children to compare the items with similar items in the United States.

PAN-AMERICAN GAMES

Sponsor a mini-Pan-American Games event. You might ask the physical education teacher to help you organize an all-school track event, soccer tournament, softball tourney, or other similar sports events. Introduce some Mexican and Central American games to the children as well. Two games are described here.

Bull in the Ring

Help the children form a large circle. Select one child to stand in the center of the circle and role-play the "bull." Have the children hold hands tightly. Then instruct the bull to try and break out of the circle by going under, over, or through the joined hands. If successful, the two children who let the bull escape must chase and tag the bull. The child who tags the bull becomes the new bull and the game continues.

Kick the Stick

Native Americans of long ago enjoyed playing this game. Designate a goal line by drawing a line with chalk or by placing a rope across the ground. Divide the class into two teams. Help the members on each team line up behind marks placed about 30 feet from the goal line. Drop a crooked stick at the feet of the first child in each line. Explain that the object of the game is for each child in turn on each team to kick the stick to the goal line and back. The stick must stay on the ground and is not to be kicked airborne. The first team to successfully have all of its members kick the stick to the goal and back is declared the winner. To increase the difficulty level, challenge the children to kick a pop bottle or bowling pin back and forth. The irregular shape makes it difficult to keep the object on a straight course!

FLAG EXTRAVAGANZA

Provide sheets of white and colored construction paper, crayons, markers, glue, and scissors for children to make flags of the countries in the Pan-American Organization of American Republics. Some of the countries are listed below. Invite the children to carry their flags in their Pan-American parade around the school. Some children might enjoy dressing in native costumes as well.

Argentina	Honduras
Bolivia	Jamaica
Brazil	Mexico
Chile	Nicaragua
Columbia	Panama
Costa Rica	Paraguay
Cuba (not active)	Peru
Dominican Republic	Trinidad
Ecuador	United States
El Salvador	Uruguay
Guatemala	Venezuela
Haiti	

PAN-AMERICAN FOOD FAIR

Food is an integral part of every Mexican and Central American fiesta. Send notes home with the children requesting parents to help their children make some Mexican and Central American foods to bring to school and share for the Pan-American Food Fair. Have parents help their children provide information like the following about the recipes they submit. Then make copies of each recipe to assemble a collection of Mexican and Central American recipes to send home with the children. Organize the recipes by region of origin.

Title of the recipe:

History of the recipe:

Supplies needed:

Ingredients:

How to make:

Serving suggestions:

On the day of the Pan-American Fiesta, cover long tables with colorful tablecloths. Make centerpieces by sticking flags that the children make of the various Pan-American countries in balls of clay wrapped in colorful sheets of tissue or cellophane.

PAN-AMERICAN CONCERT

Ask the music teacher to provide rhythm instruments and tapes or records of Mexican and Central American music. Help the children make homemade instruments as well (see the music section in the resource bank provided on pages 165-172). Play music for the children and help them listen for differences and similarities between the different music styles. Then invite the children to play along with their instruments. If possible, arrange for a guitarist to come visit the classroom and play some typical Spanish-style music for the children.

GLOBAL AWARENESS

The following questions will help the children build bridges of understanding between Mexican and Central American cultures and their own cultures.

1. Pan-American Day is celebrated throughout the Americas. How is this day celebrated in the United States?
2. Why is it important to promote goodwill and understanding between nations? What are your hopes for the future?
3. What can you do to promote world peace?

CINCO DE MAYO

May 5

In 1861, Napoleon, the emperor of France, wanting to rule Mexico, sent Archduke Ferdinand Maximillan to Mexico to serve as its emperor. The Mexicans wanted their freedom, not a ruler from France. Discontent built until, at last, on May 5, the Mexican general, Zaragoza, led a revolt against Maximillan and the French. He defeated the French in Puebla in the battle by that name. It wasn't a huge victory, but it was symbolic of what was to come. Five years later, the French were driven out and Mexico was at last free.

Every year on May 5, a mock battle takes place in Puebla to relive and remember the Mexican army for its great victory at the Battle of Puebla. This has turned into a great drama that includes uniforms, theater in the round, and half a day of exhausting acting. Interestingly, there was, at the same time as the Battle of Puebla, a small Aztec battle fought nearby. The Aztec recreate their battle in theater yearly as well.

Cinco de Mayo has become a big Mexican holiday in some parts of the United States. Americans hold parades, break piñatas, have fireworks displays, and sponsor fiestas that feature Mexican food.

CINCO DE MAYO FIESTA

Sponsor a Cinco de Mayo fiesta in your classroom. The following ideas will help make this special holiday celebration come alive for the children.

CLASSROOM ENRICHMENT ACTIVITIES

CINCO DE MAYO BATTLE

Share the book *A Treasury of Mexican Folkways* by Frances Toor with the children. (See the bibliography on pages 239-240.) Toor tells of the Cinco de Mayo event so thoroughly that you and your class will be able to easily write and present your own interpretations of the battle.

LA COCINA CHIQUITA DE PUEBLA (LITTLE PUEBLA KITCHEN)

In Puebla, a tradition for Cinco de Mayo is to make little clay replicas of Puebla kitchens. These are made by the dozens. Invite the children to make miniature Puebla kitchens. Boxes or gourds make great kitchen walls and dishes and utensils may be fashioned from baker's clay or chicle (see pages 82 and 39-40). Suggest that children make plates, cups, dishes, and food pieces, too. Miniature tea sets are also very popular in Mexico and Central America. Furniture may be carved from balsa wood and glued together with white glue as well.

MUG

MOLCAJETE AND TEJOLOTE

METATE AND MANO

PAPEL PICADO

Papel picado is a glorious paper pageantry from Puebla. Help the children make papel picado as a special tribute to Puebla (see pages 120-121). Papel picados are intricate designs cut from tissue paper that give a maximum of color and effect. Papel picado is used to create a festive atmosphere along entire streets in some Mexican and Central American communities!

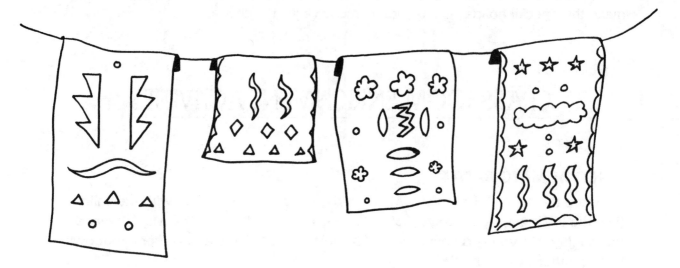

CAMOTE (SWEET POTATO CANDY)

As with other Mexican and Central American festivals, food is characteristic of the Cinco de Mayo celebration as well. Camote (sweet potato candy) has become the trademark of Puebla. Camote is decorated and packaged for gift giving or home eating. It is made and sold in dozens of shops. Ask the children to name some of their favorite candies. Ask them if they have ever eaten sweet potato candy. Then help the children make camote (see page 150). Make enough so that the children may take some home to share with family members.

SALSA PICANTE (HOT SAUCE) AND CHIPS

Mexican and Central American food is known for its spiciness. A favorite snack, both in Mexico and Central America and in the United States, is salsa picante and tortilla chips. Help the children make some salsa picante (see page 161). Invite the children to use the salsa as a dip for tortilla chips.

BONGO DRUMS

Drums are inviting instruments for children to play as part of their fiesta celebrations. Invite the children to make their own bongo drums (see page 166). Marvelous drums may be made by stretching pieces of inner tubing over large ice-cream cartons. Encourage the children to decorate the sides of the cartons in colorful designs. Some children may wish to draw scenes from the Battle of Puebla on the sides of their drums.

EL TAMBOR DE LA ALEGRÍA

El Tambor de la Alegría lends itself to drum accompaniment. Teach the children the song (see pages 209-212) and then invite them to play along on their bongo drums (see page 166).

GLOBAL AWARENESS

The following questions will help the children build bridges of understanding between Mexican and Central American cultures and their own cultures.

1. Cinco de Mayo is a celebration of victory in battle. How does the United States remember its historic battles?

2. As part of Cinco de Mayo celebrations, residents of Puebla reenact the Battle of Puebla. Does your school perform dramas for special days? Describe them.

3. Why are battles fought? Are there other ways to settle differences?

FEAST OF CORPUS CHRISTI

June

The day the Feast of Corpus Christi falls on in June varies according to the lunar calendar. The Feast of Corpus Christi honors, among other things, the arrival of the first fruits of the season in Mexico. This holiday is so blended with Native American celebrations that its flavor changes from place to place.

In the Zocolo (square) in Mexico City, this day is traditionally honored with a parade. Priests dressed in beautiful robes lead the parade followed by young men wearing crates of fruits and vegetables on their backs. People don glorious masks and young children carry little pots of herbs, small rattles, clay miniatures, and other items to encourage good spirits. The parade route is gloriously strewn with flowers.

FEAST OF CORPUS CHRISTI FIESTA

Sponsor a Feast of Corpus Christi fiesta in your classroom. The following ideas will help make this special holiday celebration come alive for the children.

CLASSROOM ENRICHMENT ACTIVITIES

FEAST OF CORPUS CHRISTI FIESTA

Ask the children if they have items at home that they consider to be good-luck tokens. Invite the children to share stories about their good-luck charms. Explain that children in Mexico and Central America carry little pots of herbs, clay miniatures, and small rattles in their Feast of Corpus Christi parade to encourage good spirits. Encourage the children to make some good-luck objects to carry in their Feast of Corpus Christi parade, such as the miniatures suggested in the following activities.

BAKER'S-CLAY MINIATURES

All over Central America, baker's clay is used to make miniatures. Children carry these miniatures in Feast of Corpus Christi parades to encourage good spirits. Help the children make a list of animals, cartoon characters, or other items that they consider to represent good luck.

Invite the children to make little clay miniatures of their favorite good-luck items (see page 82). Shapes may be cut with cookie cutters or around child-made patterns. Suggest that children decorate their miniatures with yarn, cloth, paint, or buttons and bows to give them character. White glue will hold almost anything on a flat painted surface before it is shellacked.

ECKECKO

Point out that eckeckos are clay figures that were believed by early Native Americans to bring good luck. Invite the children to make eckeckos to display in the classroom as good-luck symbols (see pages 89-91).

MULITO (DONKEY)

On the Feast of Corpus Christi, it is a tradition for children to receive mulitos (toy donkeys) as special toys. These toy donkeys are made from cornhusks or raffia. Help the children make mulitos as part of their fiesta celebration (see page 106).

PAPIER-MÂCHÉ FRUITS AND VEGETABLES

Young men carry baskets filled with fruits and vegetables on their backs in the Feast of Corpus Christi parade. Invite the children to have fun making papier-mâché fruits and vegetables to carry in their parade as well (see page 116). Have the children bring baskets from home. Tie ropes to the baskets so the baskets will hang over the children's backs.

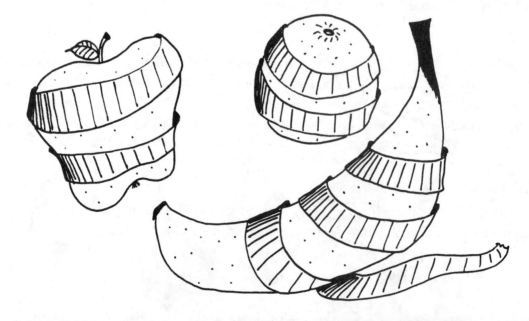

PAPIER-MÂCHÉ MASKS

The Feast of Corpus Christi is a day for masks. Encourage the children to make outrageous masks to wear in their Feast of Corpus Christi parade (see pages 117-119). Sponsor a contest for the most colorful masks, the most unusual masks, the scariest masks, and so on. Include an award for each child.

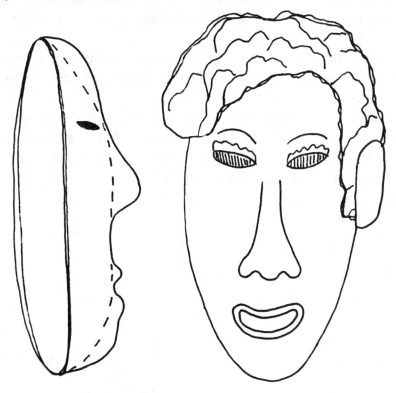

PIÑATAS

Sometimes piñatas are made in shapes that represent a given holiday, but often they are made in shapes of stars, animals, or even abstract designs. Divide the class into small cooperative-learning groups to make piñatas for the Feast of Corpus Christi (see pages 124-125).

HORCHATA (SPANISH DRINK)

Horchata is a Spanish drink enjoyed during holidays. Invite the children to make horchata for their Feast of Corpus Christi fiesta to remind them of the strong Spanish influence still alive in Mexico and Central America today (see page 156).

MARACAS

No Mexican and Central American celebration is complete without noisemakers. The Mexican and Central Americans call these special noisemakers *maracas.* Maracas are used in dancing rhythms, processionals, or just plain fun. Invite the children to make maracas from small boxes or soup cans, construction paper, dowel sticks, and garbanzo beans, pebbles, or other things that rattle (see pages 168-170).

LA PIÑATA (THE PIÑATA)

Teach the children the song *La Piñata* to sing as they break open piñatas during their Feast of Corpus Christi fiesta (see pages 215-219).

GLOBAL AWARENESS

The following questions will help the children build bridges of understanding between Mexican and Central American cultures and their own cultures.

1. The Feast of Corpus Christi is celebrated differently depending upon the region in Mexico and Central America. Are there holidays in the United States where holiday traditions are different depending upon the region where you live? Explain.

2. Noisemakers, such as maracas and marimbas, are a part of every Mexican and Central American celebration. Create a fun rhythm instrument to use in a classroom parade or celebration. Which instrument can make the loudest sound? The softest sound? The silliest sound? The most beautiful sound?

3. During the Feast of Corpus Christi, Mexicans and Central Americans believe that carrying little pots of herbs, small rattles, clay miniatures and other items encourage good spirits. What do you think would make a good classroom symbol for good luck?

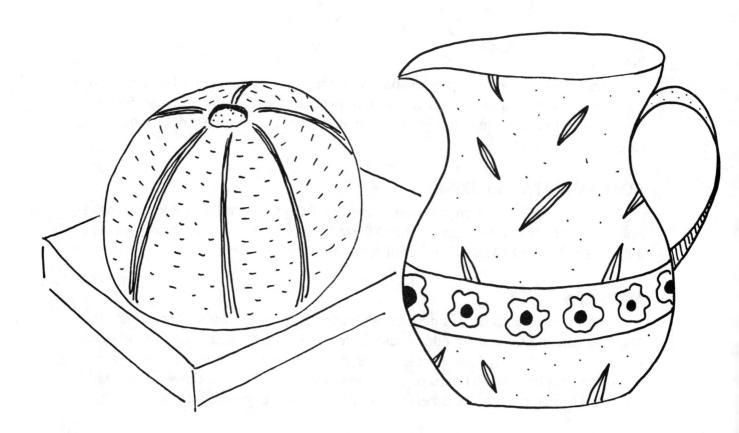

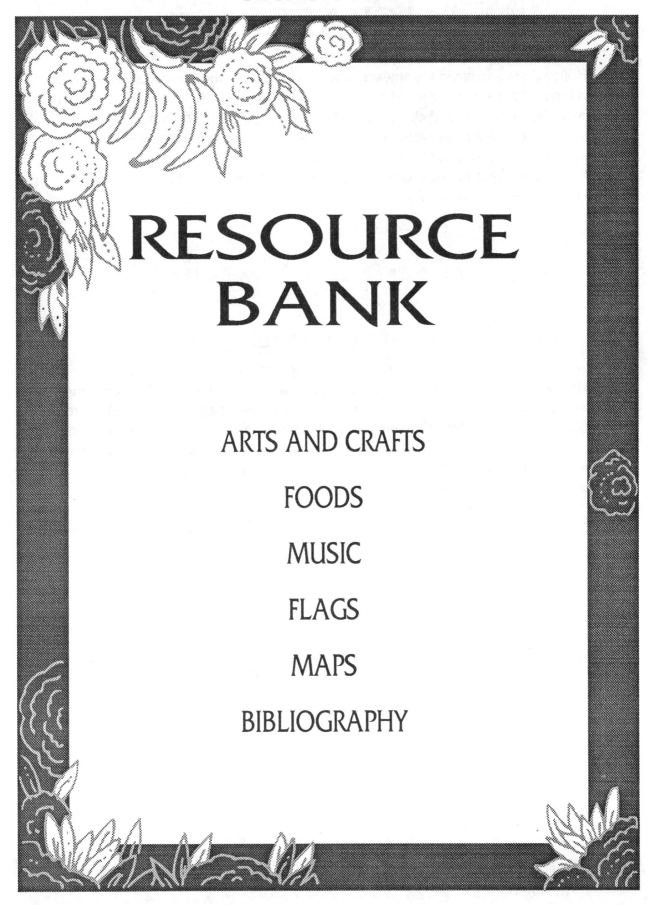

RESOURCE BANK

ARTS AND CRAFTS

FOODS

MUSIC

FLAGS

MAPS

BIBLIOGRAPHY

ARTS AND CRAFTS

Holiday arts and crafts are an excellent way of introducing the culture of a country to children. For example, the richness of the Pre-Columbian cultures varied from area to area. Feather masks and clay pots are introduced so the children may simulate some of the Pre-Columbian arts and market wares. The individuality of each region is reflected in their fiestas, food, art, music, and more.

Use the activities in this section to help children experience the uniqueness of Mexico and Central America!

ALFIÑIQUE SKULLS

Alfiñique is a strong, white, crystal-like substance widely used throughout Mexico and Central America to make miniature skulls, skeletons, coffins, and other items associated with All Souls' Day on November 2 (see page 24). Invite children to look for molds in which to make alfiñique—matchboxes make wonderful coffins and pipe cleaners bent to make fun skeletal poses may be coated with alfiñique. Have children think about other ways they might find appropriate molds as well. Encourage children to make big spooks and little spooks, or make animals of all sizes and shapes. These alfiñique creations will last a long time.

Note: If, in your judgment, this activity may be disturbing to children or parents, you might choose not to use it.

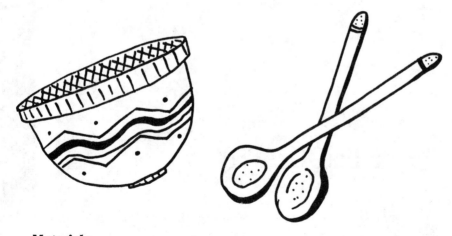

Materials:
- 2 cups granulated sugar
- 2 tsp water
- pinch of meringue powder
- mixing bowl

- spoons
- rubber balls, cut in two (candy molds and panty hose containers also make good molds for making skulls)
- petroleum jelly
- bright colors of cellophane
- pipe cleaners
- yarn
- scraps of material, buttons, bows, and beads
- scissors

1. Mix together in a bowl the sugar, water, and meringue powder to make the alfiñique.
2. Smear the two halves of the molds with petroleum jelly for easy removal of the alfiñique later.
3. Pack the alfiñique into one of the halves at a time (at least 1" deep). Remove the alfiñique from the molds when partially dry.
4. Let the molded alfiñique dry naturally for 5 hours. Or, place on a foil-covered cookie sheet that has been turned upside-down and bake in a 200° F oven for 5 minutes.
5. Remove the alfiñique from both halves of the molds.
6. Use frosting (recipe following) to "glue" the two halves together.
7. Spoon out very shallow eyes.
8. Invite children to decorate the skulls. They might glue cellophane or foil on the eyes, the hair, or elsewhere. Encourage children to sew beads to adorn the top of the skulls for hats.

Frosting
- 4 egg whites
- 2½ cups powdered sugar
- 2 tsp cream of tartar
- empty plastic egg carton
- food coloring
- electric mixer
- pastry bags (optional)

1. In a medium mixing bowl, beat 4 egg whites until they form stiff peaks.
2. Add powdered sugar and cream of tartar to the egg whites and continue beating for two minutes.
3. Divide the icing into separate plastic egg-carton sections. Add a small drop of food coloring to each section.
4. Suggest that children fill pastry bags with frosting, if they wish, and then squirt the frosting on the alfiñique to make hair and other features. This frosting is a good "glue," too. For example, if you want to attach a small bead onto a nose bone, put a bit of frosting on the nose and stick the bead in the middle.

Caution: Warn children not to eat any of the alfiñique or frosting mixtures!

AMATE PAPER

In many craft projects, Mexicans and Central Americans use a paper made from the bark of fig and mulberry trees. The fig bark makes a whitish paper, while the mulberry bark produces a darker paper. The bark is prepared by softening the fibers and then pounding the fibers into flat sheets. The sheets become useable paper when dried. Use this simulated amate paper to cover objects of all sorts. It is rather durable if given a shellac finish.

Materials:
- butcher paper or large grocery bags
- newspaper
- dry tempera paint
- electric iron
- shellac (optional)

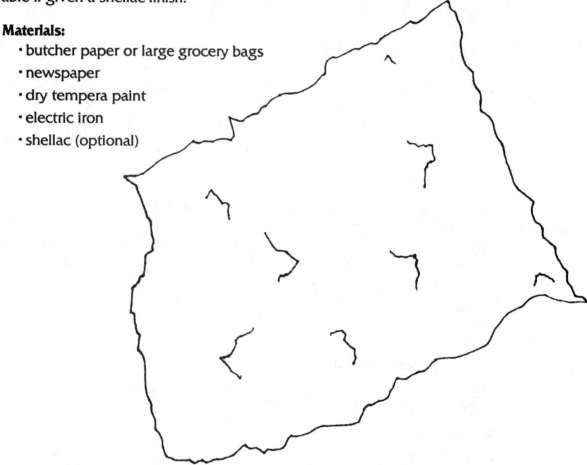

1. Crumple butcher paper or sheets cut from grocery bags.
2. Wet the crumpled paper and then spread the paper flat on newspaper. The newspaper will absorb the excess water.
3. Sprinkle dry tempera paint on the wet paper if color is desired. You may dab prepared paint on the wet paper if that is more convenient.
4. Crumple the paper again to distribute the paint. Work the paint into the cracks and creases of the paper. Some paints dry lighter, so you may need to repaint if a darker color is desired.
5. Flatten the paper to dry.
6. Use a hot iron to press the paper after it has dried.
7. Shellac the papers if children wish the colors to be more intense. Shellac will also add a bit of gloss. Be sure the room is well ventilated when using shellac.

AMATE-PAPER WITCHES (BRUJAS)

Witches are cut from amate paper either for inviting or driving out good and bad luck. The lighter colored papers are used for the good spirits and darker papers are used for the evil ones. The witch shapes have many points and protrusions that allow easy entrance and escape for the spirits! Just for fun, have children work together to make this checkerboard of witches—each, of course, being different.

Note: If, in your judgment, this activity may be disturbing to children or parents, you might choose not to use it.

Materials:
- amate paper (see page 80)
- scissors
- butcher paper
- white glue

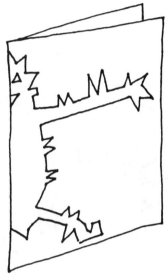

1. Fold a sheet of amate paper in half.

2. Sketch one half of a witch along the fold line. Be sure to make as many escape points or entrance points as possible.
3. Carefully cut out the witch and then unfold the paper.
4. Make a decorative panel or frieze for the classroom with butcher paper. Glue several witches in a checkerboard pattern on the paper.

BAKER'S CLAY

Baker's clay is used all over Mexico and Central America, but Ecuador has the greatest variety. Baker's clay is used to make animals, small wreaths, stars, trees, and eggs in sizes ranging from small to very large. Most of these pieces are baked until toasty brown. Use the recipe provided here to make the many Mexican and Central American projects described on the pages in this resource.

Materials:
- 4 cups flour
- 1 cup salt
- 1½ cups water
- mixing bowl

1. Mix the ingredients together with your hands in a mixing bowl until the mixture is thoroughly blended. You may wish to add food coloring to the dough (or paint the baked dough later).
2. Roll the dough out on a floured surface and cut the dough into desired shapes. Then bake the dough in an oven at a low temperature. Or, the dough may be sculpted and allowed to air dry.
3. Children may paint and decorate the clay pieces as they wish. A coat of shellac applied to the finished figures will help to preserve the pieces. Be sure the room is well ventilated when using shellac.

BAKER'S CLAY DONKEY

Invite children to make a donkey from baker's clay to remind them of Corpus Christi, a colorful Mexican holiday (see page 72)! Suggest the children try making other animals, too.

Materials:
- baker's clay
- rolling pin
- butter knife or plastic knife
- shellac
- garlic press
- heavy-duty cookie sheet
- paintbrush
- tempera paint

1. Sprinkle flour on a cookie sheet and preheat oven to 250° F.
2. Prepare a batch of baker's clay (see page 82).
3. Make a paper or cardboard pattern of a donkey.
4. Roll out the dough on a floured surface. Lay the pattern on top of the dough and then help children use a butter knife to carefully cut around the pattern.
5. An interesting texture may be applied to the donkey by using a garlic press to squirt baker's clay all over the surface.
6. Make paper patterns for flowers or other decorations children might wish to add to the donkey. Help children place these patterns on rolled out dough and cut around them as well. Arrange the decorations on the donkey. Press down firmly and then knit or etch the decorations in place with a butter knife.

7. Place the donkey on a floured cookie sheet and place in the oven to bake until done. You can check for doneness by poking a fork through the piece to check if the center is firm.
8. Cool and then invite children to paint the donkey. When the paint dries, apply a layer of shellac to preserve the donkey. Be sure the room is well ventilated when using shellac.

BASKETS

An old form of basketry used throughout the world is made from raffia-covered vegetable fibers. If palm grasses are not available in your area, strips of heavy cloth, such as denim, may be substituted. This project will result in a useful container.

Materials:
- raffia
- long, dried grasses; palm leaf strands; or pine needles
- tapestry or other large needle

1. Thread raffia through a needle.
2. Wrap the raffia around a ¼-inch grass bundle.

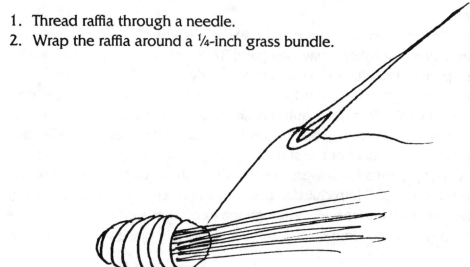

3. Coil the wrapped bundle, using the needle to tie the coils together.

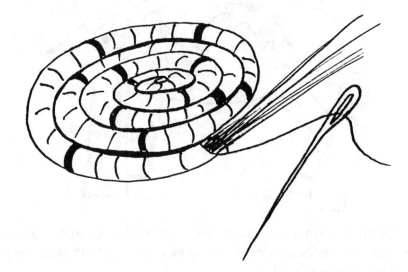

4. Keep adding grasses as they are needed to keep the coil growing.
5. Form into a bowl shape by tightening the coil as it grows larger.
6. Make handles, if desired, to sew onto the finished basket.

CLAY DOLLS

Clay is plentiful in Central America. It is used to make the many miniatures that are given to children on special festivals. When firing clay, thick pieces often explode because gases become trapped inside the clay. To prevent this from happening, use flat pieces of clay as much as possible.

Materials:
- ceramic clay
- kiln
- rolling pin
- plastic knife or toothpick
- tempera paint
- paintbrush

1. Roll out the clay to about a ⅜-inch thickness.
2. Make cone shapes with the slab. Use the scratch-slip technique to join the ends together. This is done by using a plastic knife, toothpick, or other instrument to scratch the surfaces of the edges to be joined and brushing the scratched area with slip (wet, runny clay). Join the ends of the clay together and then encourage children to use their fingers to rub the seams smooth.
3. Invite children to form the cone shapes into doll figures by pinching the tops of the cones to shape heads. They might also shape heads from clay and attach them to the cones using the scratch-slip method.

4. Fire in a kiln following firing directions provided on the clay package.
5. Have children paint on features as desired.

COIL POTS

Make clay pots using the coil method. Much of the fine Mexican and Central American pottery is made using this method. Huge vessels as well as tiny pots may be constructed in the same manner.

Materials:
- ceramic clay
- kiln
- paintbrush
- plastic knife or toothpick
- tongue depressor (or spoon)

1. Roll clay into ropes about ⅜-inch thick.
2. Help children coil the clay ropes and attach them together to build bowl shapes. Invert round-bottomed objects and place coils on these objects to get a good start on building the pots.

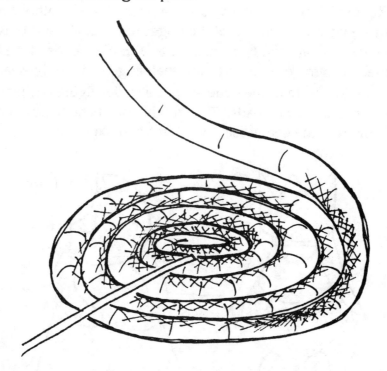

3. To make strong pots, scratch the clay ropes with a plastic knife, toothpick, or other instrument where the coils touch.
4. Brush slip (wet, runny clay) between the coil joints. While children work on new pieces, cover the clay with moist paper towels so the clay won't dry. You may also slow the drying process by placing the piece in a refrigerator.
5. Show the children how to press the coils together and smooth the surfaces with a flat stick or spoon. If the coils become too soft as children start their pots, stop and let the clay rest until it becomes firmer. When finished, the lines between the coils should be invisible.

6. If they wish, children may attach handles using the scratch-slip technique.
7. To make a closed pot, as shown here, make two bowl shapes. When the pots are leather hard, join them together using the scratch-slip technique.

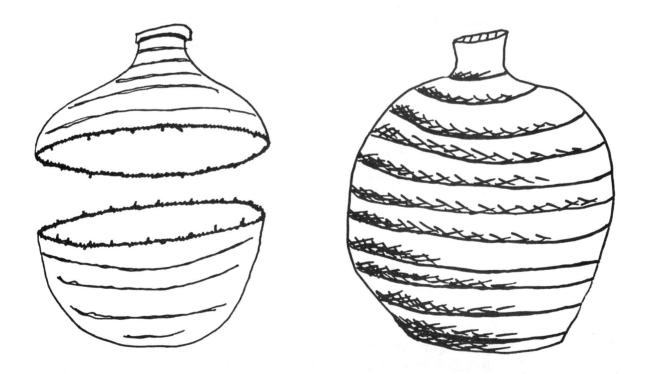

8. Fire in a kiln following firing directions provided on the clay package.

CROSS-STITCH EMBROIDERY

Much of the embroidery done by Pre-Columbian groups was of the plants and animals that made up their environment. Using yarns that were naturally dyed, the Maya and other Native Americans were able to create colorful designs distinctive of their tribes.

Materials:
- quadrille graph paper
- pencil
- monk's cloth or burlap
- yarn
- needle

1. Have children draw several designs or pictures on quadrille paper by X-ing out squares.

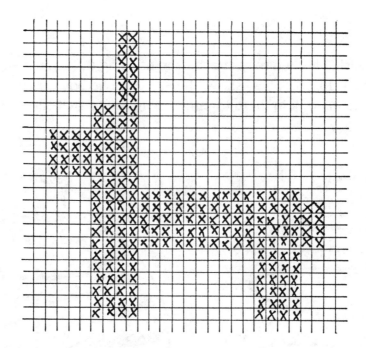

2. Invite children to choose their favorite designs or pictures.
3. Count the number of squares wide and long their designs or pictures are. Add a few squares to each measurement to allow for borders for framing.
4. Cut a piece of monk's cloth or burlap to size for each design.
5. Thread needles with the color yarn the children wish to use. Help children cross-stitch their designs or pictures. Have children start at the widest part of their pictures to make sure the pictures fit on the cloth.
6. Encourage children to experiment using more than one color of yarn.

ECKECKO

Eckeckos are used for good luck. Invite the children to make good luck eckeckos. An eckecko can be made from cardboard or clay.

Materials:
- cardboard
- tempera paint
- glue
- paintbrush
- scissors
- shellac
- 4 cups flour
- 1 cup salt
- 1½ cups water
- mixing bowl
- rolling pin
- plastic knife
- cookie sheet

Cardboard Eckecko

1. Invite children to trace the eckecko pattern provided on page 91 on a sheet of cardboard or tagboard.
2. Have children cut out the pattern and then paint the doll with bright colors.
3. When the paint is dry, bend the hands and elbows as indicated.

4. Hang miniatures of objects, or pictures of objects, on the eckecko's arms and hands.

Clay Eckecko

1. Sprinkle flour on a cookie sheet and preheat the oven to 250° F.
2. Mix the ingredients for baker's clay (see page 82) together in a mixing bowl with your hands until the mixture is thoroughly blended.
3. Place the dough on a floured surface. Cut out the eckecko pattern provided on page 91 and place it on the dough. Help children use a plastic knife to cut around the pattern.
4. Invite children to make any features or other details they might like to add to the eckecko from clay and then press them firmly on the clay figure. Use a plastic knife to scratch or etch the clay pieces to the figure.
5. Place the eckecko on the cookie sheet. Bend the elbows and hands as indicated on the pattern. You might also insert thin pieces of wire along the arms and hands of each eckecko to hang them when finished.
6. Bake the eckecko until done. You can check for doneness by poking a fork through the pieces and making sure the center is firm.
7. Invite the children to paint the baked eckecko once it has cooled. When the paint dries, apply a layer of shellac to preserve the eckecko. Be sure the room is well ventilated when using shellac.

8. Hang miniatures of objects, or pictures of objects, on the eckecko's arms and hands.

Eckecko Pattern

FEATHER MASKS

Feather masks are marvelous disguises to wear. You can find brightly colored feathers at most craft stores. Invite children to make feather masks to wear at their next fiesta celebration! Encourage children to try wearing the masks inverted, with the eyes slanting up or down!

Materials:
- tagboard
- thin elastic
- variety of feathers
- sequins and spangles
- scissors
- metallic decorative tape
- glue

1. Trace and cut out the mask pattern provided on page 93. Help children trace the pattern on a sheet of tagboard.
2. Pierce a hole in each side of each mask. Attach a length of elastic to fit around each child's head.
3. Invite the children to glue a variety of feathers all over the masks in interesting designs.

4. Encourage children to glue sequins or spangles on the feather-covered masks to emphasize features. Metallic decorative tape looks especially dramatic when used to outline the eye holes.

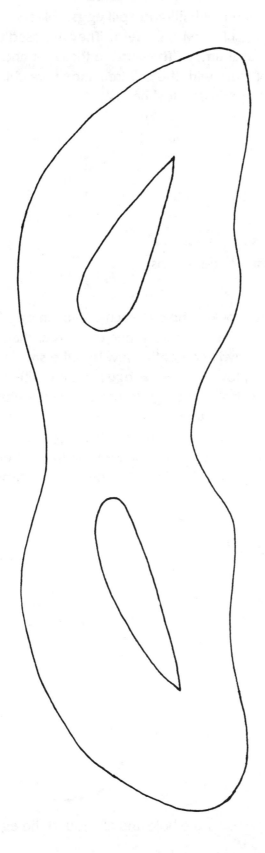

FILL-AND-SPILL EGGS

Children will have lots of fun with fill-and-spill eggs! Fill-and-spill eggs are eggs emptied of their contents and filled with confetti. They are used throughout Mexico and Central America for festival times. They add to the color and celebration spirit of any occasion. Make lots of them with the children and invite children to have fun breaking them open over their classmates' heads!

Materials:
- eggs
- needle
- bowl
- confetti
- paper punch or scissors (optional)
- brightly colored tissue-paper scraps
- white glue

1. Use a needle to gently poke a hole in each end of an egg (be sure eggs are at room temperature). Make the hole in one end larger than the other.
2. Hold the egg over a bowl and gently blow into the smaller hole until the insides have all been blown out of the eggs and into the bowl. (You may need to prick the yolk inside the egg to break it before blowing.)
3. Let the eggshell dry thoroughly.
4. Use a needle to enlarge the bigger hole in the eggshell so that the empty egg may be loosely filled with confetti. Children can make their own confetti with a paper punch or scissors and sheets of colored tissue paper.

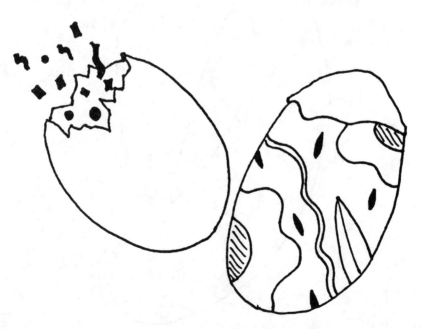

5. Then glue tissue paper over the hole and all around the eggshell for decoration.

PAPER FLOWERS

Flowers are always in bloom everywhere in Mexico and Central America. Invite children to make lots of paper flowers for their Mexican and Central American fiestas. Stick them in pots or baskets. Children might also wish to attach the flowers to wire that can then be fastened onto tables or desks. Suggest that children stick some flowers behind their ears, too!

Materials:
- crepe-paper bolt
- scissors
- 24-28 gauge wire (soft)
- flower tape (optional)

1. Fold one section of paper from a crepe-paper bolt in half the long way and then in half again.

2. Cut four pointed petals at one time.

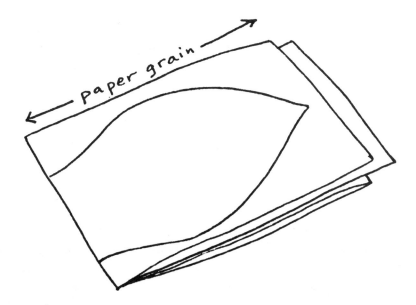

3. Then fold two more sections of paper from a crepe-paper bolt in half the long way twice. Cut 8 broad, rounded petals at one time.

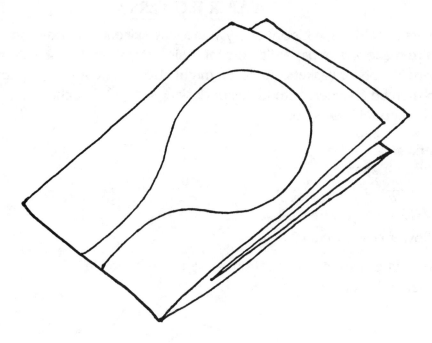

4. Separate all of the cut petals.
5. Gently stretch the widest part of each pointed petal only. For each rounded petal, gently stretch the widest part of the petal in one direction and the top part in the other.

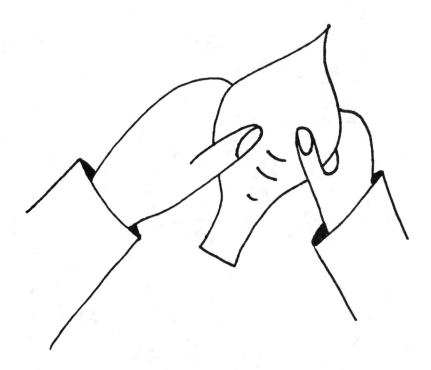

6. Use the petals to start forming a flower. Roll the four pointed petals gently into a cylinder. Grasp the base of the petals firmly. Make sure that each petal overlaps the edge of the previous petal and that the flat part of each petal is even.

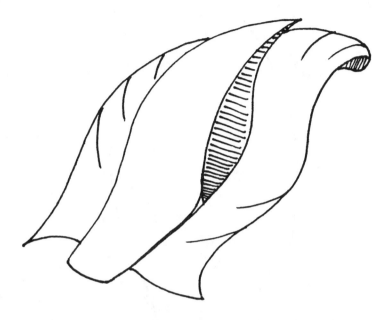

7. Add the eight round petals, one at a time, in the same manner.
8. When all twelve petals are assembled, twist a piece of soft wire around the base. If you wish, cover the wire and the base of the petals with floral tape.
9. Gently open the petals and adjust them to resemble a real flower.

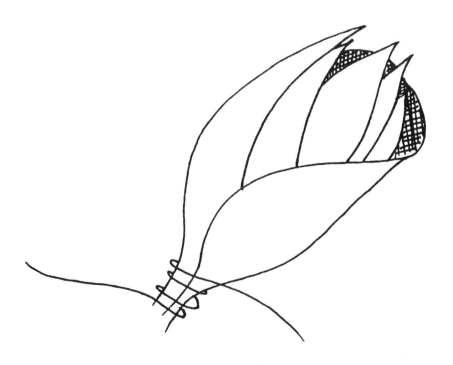

Paper Flower Patterns

GOD'S EYES (OJOS DE DIOSES)

These colorful decorations can be made from straight sticks, tree limbs, or branches. Invite children to experiment!

Materials:
- yarn scraps
- popsicle sticks (or other straight sticks)

1. Cross two sticks at the center at right angles.

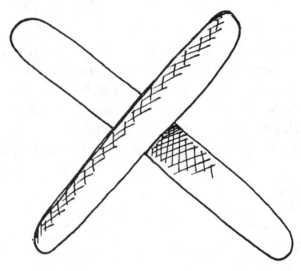

2. Ask children to tie yarn scraps together to make continuous strings.
3. Help children wrap a length of yarn around the centers of the two sticks to reinforce the cross.
4. Then show children how to begin wrapping the yarn around the individual arms of the sticks, connecting the sticks with yarn.
5. Encourage children to keep weaving more scraps of yarn on the sticks until you have a decorative piece.

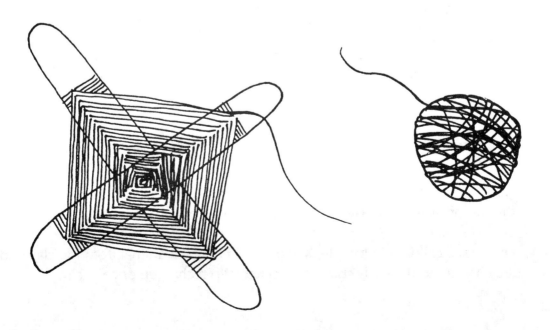

HAIRY CHIA ARMADILLO

Animal planters are lots of fun to make! Invite children to experience watching seeds sprout and grow. Although you can buy chia-animal planters at most large department stores, making clay animals in class is a delightful and valuable experience. Ask the art teacher to fire the children's clay animals in a kiln. Look for chia seeds at health food stores.

Materials:
- clay
- chia seeds

1. Invite children to make animal shapes from clay. First use the coil method to make two bowls (see page 86). These will form the main sections of the bodies. The animals needs a hollow center to hold water.

2. Fasten the two bowls together using the scratch-slip technique. Scratch the surfaces of the clay pieces where they are to be joined. Put the two pieces together and then smooth slip (wet, runny clay) over the joint.

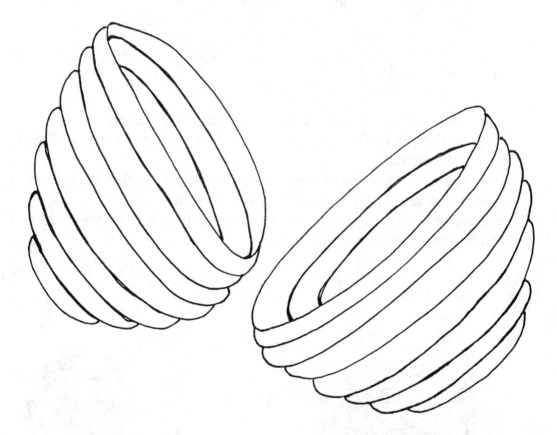

3. Help children use a thick dowel stick or their fingers to make small holes in the top of each chia body so that water may be poured into the planters each day.

4. Encourage children to form legs and a head for each animal from the clay and attach them to the body using the scratch-slip technique once again.

5. Bisque (or first) fire the clay animals. After the firing, fill the animals with water through the small holes in the tops of each animal body. Because the bisqued clay will not be waterproof, be sure to place the animal planters on a waterproof surface.

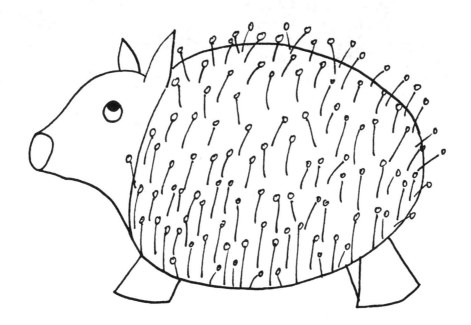

6. Soak chia seeds in a bowl of water for a few minutes until they become gummy and sticky. Help children apply the seeds to the outside of their clay animals. In a few weeks, the animals will sprout chia hair! Keep water in the clay animals and see how long their chia hair will grow!

LOCAL COLOR

Fabric-making and embellishments are a part of Mexican and Central American history. The early Native Americans used natural dyes to color their own yarn and cloth for weaving and sewing. Many plants that people consider "weeds" yield beautiful colors when boiled. Discover the color in the plants in your area!

Materials:

- grasses, berries, blossoms, and other colorful plants
- 1 gallon water
- salt
- yarns to dye (cotton yarn works best)
- cotton fabric
- large enamel pan for each color
- stove, hot plate, or electric skillet
- large ladle or spoon

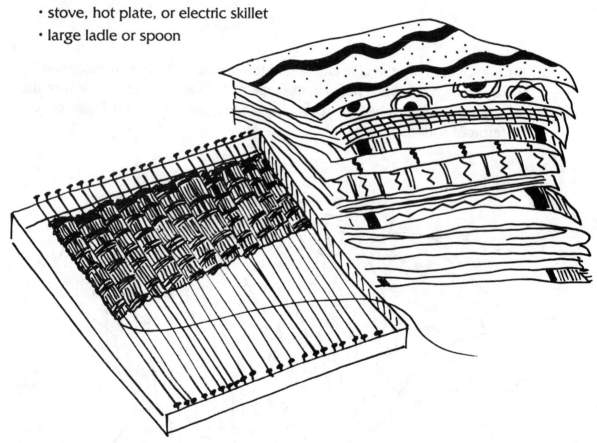

1. Mix together the grasses, berries, blossoms, and other plants, along with salt and water, in a large pot over medium heat.
2. Bring to a boil and then boil for 10 minutes.
3. Remove the fibers. Gently add yarn and cloth to the mixture in the pot. Simmer for 10 minutes, stirring vigorously.
4. Remove the yarn and cloth and hang them on a line to dry. Protect the floor with newspaper or a sheet of plastic.

MIGAJON

Migajon is a modeling clay made from bread. Use it in place of baker's clay to make toy miniatures or other projects.

Materials:
- 8 slices day-old white bread (cut into cubes, with crusts removed)
- ½ cup white glue
- mixing bowl
- food coloring
- rolling pin
- skewer
- plastic knife
- miniature cookie cutters
- tempera paint
- paintbrushes

1. Mix the bread and glue together thoroughly in a mixing bowl. Add food coloring as desired.
2. Knead the dough for 5 minutes on a floured surface. Add flour as the dough becomes shinier.
3. Children may either roll the dough out on a floured surface and cut out shapes with cookie cutters, using a plastic knife, or model the dough by hand. Popular miniatures to make in Mexico and Central America are tea sets, little burros, small people, animals, and food pieces.
4. If children are making beads or hanging pieces, carefully poke a skewer through the pieces and then slide the skewer out quickly again to keep the hole from closing.
5. Air dry the pieces and then invite children to paint and decorate as desired.

MOLAS

Molas are primarily made in Panama. A mola is an intricate applique craft that looks extremely complicated. Turtles, fish, cats, and free-form shapes seem to be the most popular themes for the designs. You may want to have children start with simple designs at first.

Materials:
- 2 pencils
- rubberbands
- construction paper in a variety of colors
- newspaper
- X-acto knife

1. On a sheet of brightly colored construction paper, invite children to draw a simple design, such as a flower, animal, or other item found in nature.

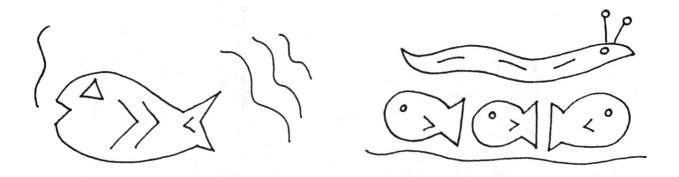

2. Double all of the lines. (An easy way to do this is to draw with two pencils fastened together with rubberbands.)

3. Use several thicknesses of newspaper (20 layers or so) as a cutting board. Cut out all spaces that do *not* fall between the double lines with an X-acto knife, leaving skeleton-like figures.

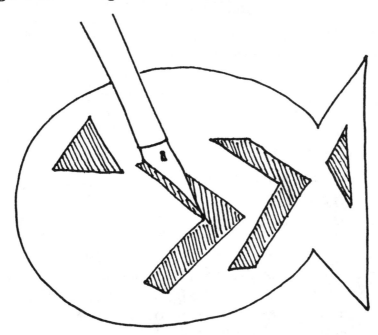

4. Have children glue the cutout figures onto contrasting colors of construction paper. Black will leave an interesting outline around the first colored form.
5. Place the glued figures on the layers of newspaper again and then use the X-acto knife to cut as shown along the dotted lines, leaving a border of the second colored paper showing.

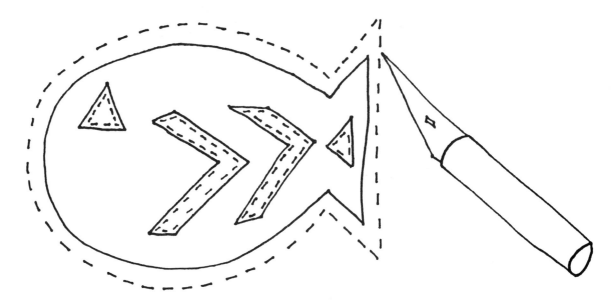

6. Continue again if desired. Paste onto a final background color when children are finished for mounting.
7. If you wish to repeat an abstract design, fold a lightweight sheet of pattern paper into fourths. Draw the design, unfold, and transfer the design to colored construction paper. Double all of the lines.

MULITO (DONKEY)

Invite children to make Corpus Christi mulitos from cornhusks. A mulito is a traditional toy made for the June festival (see page 72).

Materials:
- cornhusks
- straw (or cloth)
- masking tape
- palm fronds or thin cornhusk strip
- cornstalks or sticks
- aniline (or another stain)
- paintbrush

1. Help each child form a rough shape of a donkey's body (no legs) from cloth or straw. Use masking tape to hold the form's shape.
2. Wrap cornhusks tightly around the cloth or straw body shapes. Tie with twisted grasses or thin cornhusk strips.
3. Cut pieces of cornstalk or sticks to insert into the bodies as legs.

4. Paint the assembled donkey with aniline or other similar stains.

MURAL MAKING

Painting a mural can be a big undertaking. The following techniques will help students work together to get the mural done quickly and still do a great job of covering a topic. Painting with large paintbrushes will also make the work progress quickly!

Materials:
- sheet of paper
- colored pencils
- butcher paper (cut to cover one wall)
- tempera paint
- 2-inch paintbrushes

1. Define with the children the topic of the mural, such as Costa Rican people, Guatemalan crafts, history of Honduras, and so on.
2. Ask children to brainstorm ideas that might be included in the mural.
3. Have the children draw their ideas or designs for the mural on pieces of paper first.
4. As a class, invite the children to select the ideas or design drawings to be used on the mural. Every design may not be needed.
5. Decide if there might be a background motif to tie the theme and drawings together.
6. Invite the children to paint the background first, using large brushes. Flow pens work well for fast detail work.
7. Then assign each child a space on the mural to first draw and then paint his or her ideas or designs.

NEARIKAS

Use this technique to create beautiful nature drawings just like the Huichol of long ago. Beeswax may be purchased in most craft stores, from beekeepers, or by melting candles.

Materials:
- piece of wood or masonite (about 4" x 6")
- yarn scraps
- beeswax
- blunt knife

1. Soften the beeswax in a low oven (or place it in the sun) until it is somewhat pliable.
2. Spread a 1/16" layer of wax on warmed pieces of wood or masonite. Smooth the layer as much as possible.
3. Have children draw nature designs, such as animal shapes, on sheets of paper the same size as the pieces of wood.
4. Transfer the designs onto the wood by first placing the designs face down on the waxed wood. Then help children trace over their designs with a blunt pencil, exerting a small amount of pressure so the designs will be pressed into the soft wax.
5. Help children use a blunt knife to press yarn into the wax beneath each design. Keep going around and around inside the design until all of the inside area is filled. Keep the yarn strands as close together as possible.
6. Cover each different area of the design with a contrasting color of yarn. Cover every part of the beeswax surface!

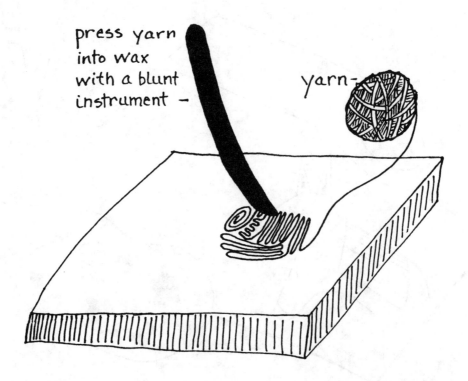

press yarn into wax with a blunt instrument —

yarn —

OFRENDAS

Invite children to use their creative talents to fashion glorious little shrines to celebrate All Soul's Day (see page 24)! Encourage children to decorate these with as many different items as they wish.

Note: If, in your judgment, this activity may be disturbing to children or parents, you might choose not to use it.

Materials:
- boxes, large and small
- tempera paint
- paintbrushes
- paper flowers, fruit (real or artificial), candles, and other decorative items
- glue

1. Help each child paint several different-size boxes and arrange them so that a larger box is between two smaller boxes to resemble a small shrine.
2. Glue the painted boxes together.
3. Invite children to decorate their "shrines" as imaginatively as possible—with paper flowers, fruit, candles, fancy materials, and so on.

OX CART

Costa Ricans take great pride in decorative ox carts. Carts are painted with designs that are unique to each family. The designs are handed down from generation to generation, much like a coat of arms! Help children make replicas of these carts. Invite children to create unique designs to represent their families.

Materials:
- small boxes
- cardboard
- white glue
- brass fasteners
- pencils
- red, blue, black, green, yellow tempera paint
- paintbrushes
- scissors

1. For each cart, cut eight cardboard posts to glue to the outside of a box.
2. Cut a tongue for each cart from cardboard. Help each child fasten a tongue to his or her box with brass fasteners.
3. Cut four circles from cardboard for the wheels. Glue the circles together in pairs to make the wheels strong. Place a heavy book on top of the glued wheels to keep them flat while they dry.
4. Cut little holes in the center of the wheels and in the sides of the cart where the wheels will be attached.
5. Push a pencil through the holes in the cart for an axle and then slide the wheels on.
6. Make hubcaps from papier-mâché or heavy cardboard.
7. Cut a seat for the cart from cardboard. Bend the ends and glue in place.
8. Invite children to paint beautiful designs on their finished carts.

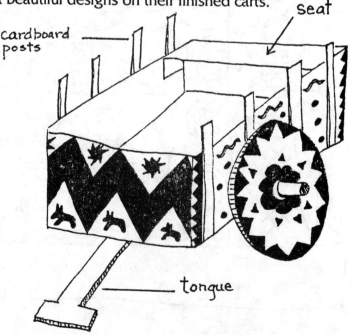

cardboard posts

seat

tongue

PALM PIECES

Palm leaves are used by Mexican and Central Americans to create art pieces. During special events, these imaginative pieces are carried in processions. Encourage students to try their hands at weaving.

Materials:
- palm leaves
- white glue
- clothespins
- wax paper

1. Show children how to weave every other frond of a palm over the other to create interesting designs.

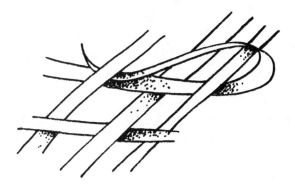

2. Glue the end tips in place. Use a clothespin to clamp the glued spots until dry (place wax paper between the clothespin and the palm).

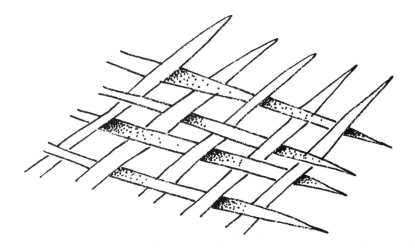

3. Palm fronds not attached to the stem may be woven and fastened with glue as shown here.

PAPIER-MÂCHÉ

Papier-Mâché is inexpensive and easy to make. This process is used in Mexico and Central America, as well as the United States, for making all sorts of sturdy craft pieces, such as masks, stick horses, bowls, maracas, piggy banks, skeletons, skulls, and other art forms made to delight.

Materials:
- newspaper (use a variety of colors)
- facial tissue
- paper towels
- old sheeting and other fabric (makes a tough papier-mâché)
- scissors
- liquid starch (mix ½ cup white glue with ½ cup water or boiled corn starch)
- masking and cellophane tape
- petroleum jelly (for easy removal)
- wax paper (for a work area that's easy to clean)

Paints:
- tempera or poster paint mixed with canned milk for durability

Decorations:
- cloth
- buttons
- sequins
- feathers

Kinds of Papier-Mâché:

Mash

Tear up small pieces of newspaper or facial tissue. Soak the pieces in liquid starch or other liquid adhesive. Squeeze out the liquid and form the paper mass into the desired shape. Then let the shape dry. Mash is usually used to strengthen other papier-mâché pieces. Mash is also well suited for making figures of pearls, rubies, and other small jewels. Glitter may be stuck right in the mash!

Strip

Strips of papier-mâché materials are used to retain and define a shape. For example, strips of newspaper or cloth can be dipped in the papier-mâché paste and then used to cover an inflated balloon. When the papier-mâché is dry, the balloon is popped and the papier-mâché can be decorated or made into a piñata.

Finishes:

Antiquing

Make a very strong mixture of instant coffee. Dip a rag in the coffee and wipe it over the painted papier-mâché surface. Be sure to wipe the coffee in all of the small crevices! Let the finish dry. Repeat if needed.

Smooth and Shiny

Brush mayonnaise or a beaten egg over a painted or antiqued surface as a substitute for shellac.

Forever Paint

Add 2 tablespoons powered milk to 1 cup tempera paint. This paint won't come off!

ALL SOULS' DAY FIGURES

Help children make some scary figures just for fun! Children can create little skeleton figures doing their favorite things—riding horses, playing ball, reading a book, and so on. Suggest children make big sombreros or other outrageous clothing for the skeletons to wear. Encourage children to be creative!

Note: If, in your judgment, this activity may be disturbing to children or parents, you might choose not to use it.

Materials:
- wheat paste
- ½" newspaper strips
- newspaper, foil, or paper tubes
- paper towels
- facial tissues
- paintbrush
- tempera paint
- masking tape
- shellac

1. Help children crumple paper or foil into balls. Then show the children how to form the balls into doll shapes. Use masking tape to hold the shapes together. Cardboard tubes may be used as a base for each doll as well.

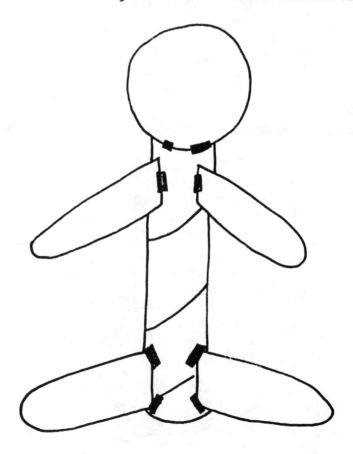

2. Have children dip strips of newspaper into wheat paste. Show children how to squeeze the excess paste from the strips and then smooth the strips onto the doll forms. Repeat with other colors or kinds of paper (comics, paper towels, and so on) to be sure the doll forms are completely covered. Apply at least 3 or 4 layers.

3. Build features with mash (see page 112). Press the features on firmly. Decorate with mash stripes, dots, or ripples (or glue yarn or buttons on the dolls) for interest and for texture.
4. Make the figures in different poses.
5. Smooth the doll forms by applying a final coat of paper-towel strips.
6. Let the papier-mâché dry for two days before painting.
7. Paint bones on the figures. Then apply a coat of shellac when the paint dries. Be sure the room is well ventilated when using shellac.
8. Glue scraps of tissue, raffia, yarn, feathers, or other materials on the doll for special effects.

FRUITS AND VEGETABLES

Papier-mâché fruits and vegetables may be made by using real fruits or vegetables as molds. Use the papier-mâché objects to recreate Pre-Columbian markets or as decorations.

Materials:
- wheat paste
- real fruits and vegetables
- petroleum jelly
- ½" newspaper strips
- paper towels or facial tissues
- paintbrush
- tempera paint
- shellac

1. Cover fruits and vegetables with petroleum jelly.
2. Have children dip strips of newspaper into wheat paste. Show children how to remove the excess paste and then use the strips to cover the fruits and vegetables. Apply 4 to 5 layers of strips on each piece of fruit. Make one layer paper-toweling or facial-tissue strips. Alternate the direction of each layer for added strength.

3. Allow the papier-mâché to dry thoroughly.
4. Cut the papier-mâché objects in half. Remove the fruits and vegetables.
5. Glue the papier-mâché forms back together and then invite the children to paint the objects. Brush shellac on the objects once the paint dries for durability. Be sure the room is well ventilated when using shellac.

MASKS

Masks encourage children to pretend to be anything or anyone they wish to be! There are a number of ways to make masks. In parts of Mexico and Central America, masks are extremely well-made. Masks have special significance in many holiday celebrations.

Materials:
- clay or plastacine (about 4 lbs)
- papier-mâché
- newspaper strips
- petroleum jelly
- masking tape
- scissors
- tempera paint
- paintbrushes
- shellac

To make super-fine masks:

1. Use a large handful of clay for each mask. Place the clay on a flat surface. Have children model the clay into the shape of a face for the mask they wish to make. Place the face shapes over wadded up newspaper for added support.
2. Smear petroleum jelly over the clay faces (both sides) to make it easier to remove from the paper.
3. Arrange a layer of dry paper over the shaped features. Tape the paper around the bottom of the clay bases to hold them in place.
4. Use papier-mâché strips to cover the clay bases. Apply at least 3 layers of strips. Alternate the direction of each layer for strength.

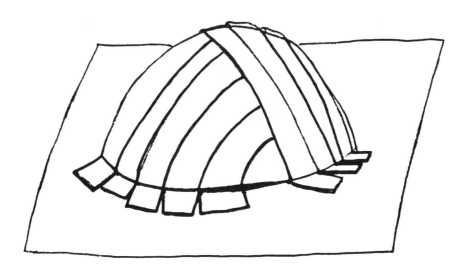

5. Use mash (see page 112) to add extra details, such as eyebrows and ears.

6. Allow the masks to dry thoroughly (about two days).

7. Remove the dried masks from the clay bases and trim the edges with scissors.

8. Invite children to paint their masks in brilliant colors and decorate with a variety of materials. Then shellac the entire mask to preserve it. "Hair" (yarn) may be glued to the mask once the shellac dries. Be sure the room is well ventilated when using shellac.

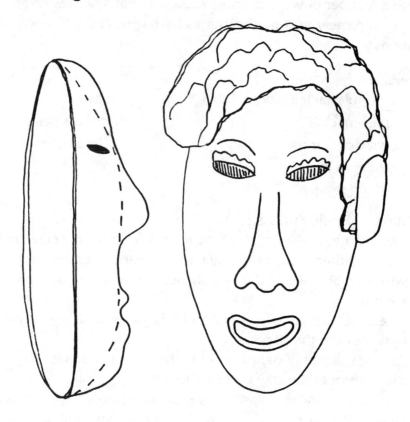

To make quicker, less smooth masks:

1. Fill paper sacks with newspaper and then tie the bags shut. Invite the children to form the bags into the approximate shapes of faces. Use masking tape to hold the shapes together. It will be easier to handle if the shaped bags are also taped to a flat surface.

2. Help children try to make the shapes as smooth as possible. Arrange one layer of dry newspaper strips on the bases.
3. Apply papier-mâché strips over the entire surface. Repeat until there are at least 3 to 4 layers over the entire base. Alternate the direction of each layer for strength.

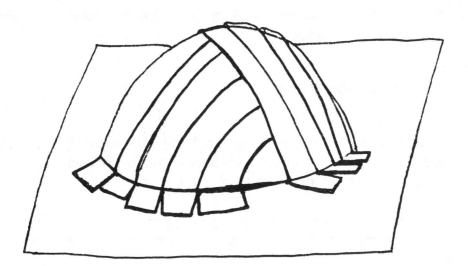

4. Build up features by putting small balls of paper under more pasted strips. The last layer may be facial tissue or paper-toweling to make painting easier.

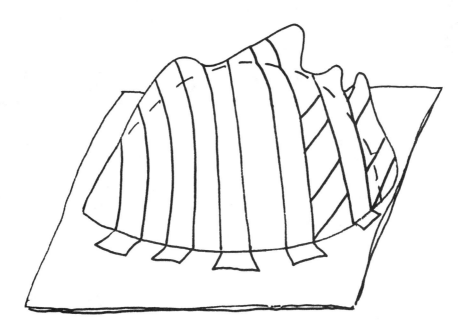

5. Allow the masks to dry for two or more days and then cut around the edges. Remove the crumpled paper inside.
6. Have children decorate their masks with paint and scraps of tissue, raffia, yarn, feathers, or cloth. Then shellac. "Hair" (yarn) may be glued on the mask once the shellac dries. Be sure the room is well ventilated when using shellac.

PAPEL PICADO

For festive Mexican and Central American occasions, tissue-paper sheets cut into intricate designs are often used to brighten a room. These cut-paper pieces are strung on a cord or wire much like wash on a line! Experimentation is the only way of mastering this art. Be patient!

Materials:

- tissue paper in lots of bright colors
- scissors
- string
- paste

1. Spread sheets of tissue paper flat. Fold down the top edges about ½ inch and tape the edges down. Leave a space near the fold of each paper so a wire may be strung through for hanging.

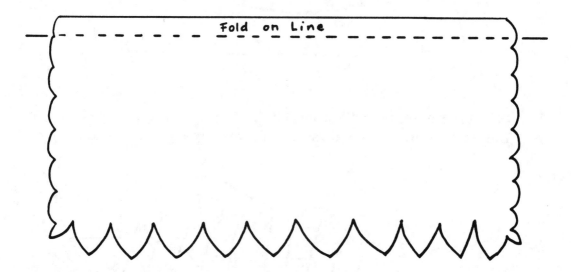

2. Fold the papers in half. Help children carefully cut out designs along the folded edges.

3. Fold the paper in half a second time and cut more designs along the folded edge. (Experimentation is the only way of mastering this technique!)

4. String the tissue-paper cutouts on a wire or string that has been hung across the classroom.

PIGGY BANKS

These piggy banks double as wonderful noisemakers for Mexican and Central American fiestas! Encourage children to think of other animals to make as well.

Materials:
- unwaxed paper cups (2 for each child)
- coins, beans, or other small, hard objects
- masking tape
- wheat paste
- ½" newspaper strips
- tempera paint
- shellac
- paintbrushes
- small, round sticks (or cut dowel sticks)
- scissors

1. Give each child two paper cups. Have children put several coins or other objects inside one of their paper cups. Tape another paper cup to the cup, top-to-top.

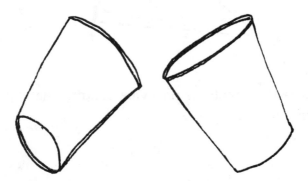

2. Cut a coin slot along the middle of one side of the cups.

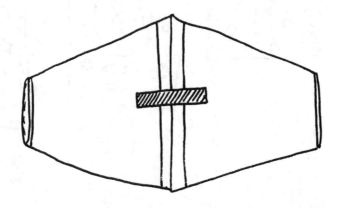

3. Make 4 small leg holes near the ends of the cups on the sides opposite the coin slots.

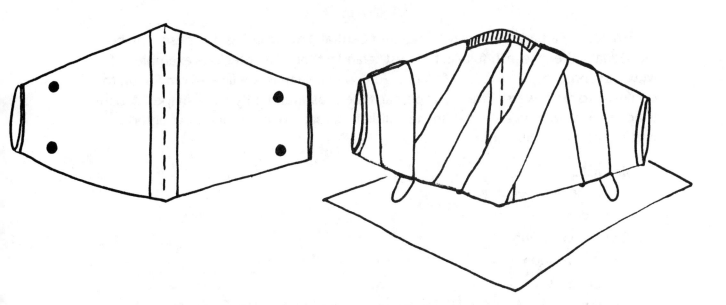

4. Invite children to cover the cups with papier-mâché strips. Make sure the children do not cover the coin slots or leg holes! Make one end of each bank more pointed for a nose.

5. Insert sticks into the leg holes.
6. Dry for several days.
7. Encourage children to paint their piggy banks with flower designs or other decorations to make the piggy banks festive.

PIÑATAS

Piñatas are a part of every Mexican and Central American fiesta. These may be individually the loveliest, funniest, silliest, grandest, or most precious examples of Mexican and Central American folk art. Any, or all, shapes are fine—from Santa, to donkeys, to fat flowers! The star is perhaps the most frequently used shape. A party is not a party without a piñata! Invite children to make one for their next birthday party or other celebration!

Materials:
- ½" newspaper strips
- wheat paste
- tempera paint
- large balloon
- paintbrushes
- crepe paper, tissue, feathers, beads, or other decorative materials
- strong cord or wire
- scissors or knife

1. Inflate and tie a large balloon.

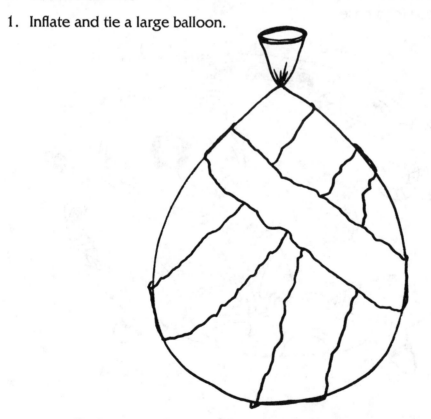

2. Invite children to apply newspaper strips dipped in wheat paste all over the surface of the balloon. Use different colors of newspaper (comics, sports, ads) for each layer. Apply each layer in a different direction to make it easier to tell if you have covered the entire surface of the balloon. Apply no more than 3 layers or the balloon will be too difficult to break open later.

3. Add features and details, such as a head and legs, with wads of paper or paper cups covered with papier-mâché strips. Mash (see page 112) may be used to make facial features, bumps, and other surface texture details.

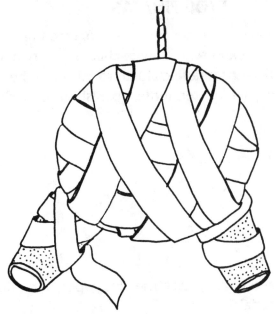

4. Let the figure dry for several days.
5. Cut an opening in the top or bottom of the piñata and pop and remove the balloon inside.
6. Fill the cavity of the piñata with goodies, such as candies, unshelled peanuts, tangerines, toy trinkets, and other items, and then close the opening with a bit of tape or tissue.
7. Punch two small holes in the top of the piñata and insert a strong cord or coat hanger wire as a hanger for the piñata.
8. Invite the children to paint the piñata and then decorate it as they wish—with tissue paper, crepe paper, or whatever their imaginations allow!

FROG PIÑATAS

The Mexican artist has all sorts of innovative ways of creating specialty piñatas that are sturdy enough to swing and sway. Invite children to try making these frog piñatas. But don't stop there—encourage children to think of other creatures or items to make as well. Perhaps a rooster, turtle, Spanish galleon, donkey, or hippo!

Materials:
- ½" newspaper strips
- wheat paste
- tempera paint
- clay pots
- cardboard
- paintbrushes
- crepe paper (or colored tissue paper, metallic paper, yarn, ribbons, velvet, and other similar materials)
- small boxes
- strong cord or wire
- scissors
- glue
- goodies, such as candy, fruit, or nuts

1. For each frog piñata, tie a length of cord or wire around the middle of a popsicle stick. Insert the wire through the hole in the bottom of each clay pot (from the inside).

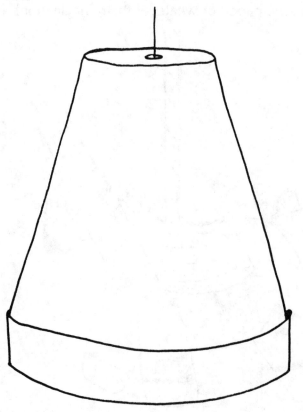

2. Fill the pots with goodies. Tape sturdy sheets of cardboard across the opening. Then have children cover the pots with several layers of papier-mâché strips to make the basic shape of a frog.

3. Attach small boxes as legs for the frogs. Or, shape rolled or crumpled paper or foil into leg shapes. Use pasted strips to glue the "legs" to the bases.

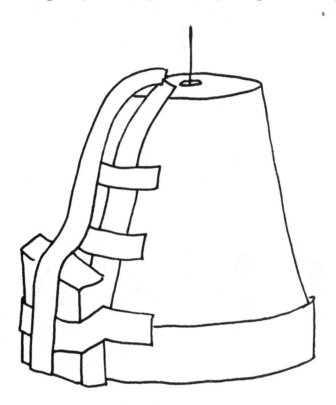

4. Invite children to use mash (see page 112) to form eyes, warts, or other details to make the frogs more interesting. Let the papier-mâché dry completely.

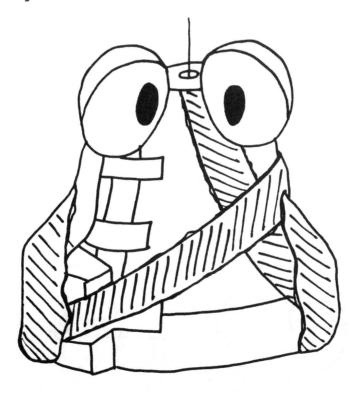

5. Encourage children to paint their piñatas and then decorate them. Fringe fifteen 3' strips of crepe paper or tissue paper for each frog piñata. Curl the ends and let them flutter (make deeper cuts for fluffier fringe). Glue the fringe in layers on each piñata. Foil eyes, feather lashes, yarn braid, and a hundred other surprises will make the children's piñatas the pride of Mexico and Central America!

SAILING SHIPS

Children can make lots of shapes by folding paper in unique ways. Encourage children to try making these sailing ships. You might use the ships to help tell the story of Columbus' adventures to the Americas. Get a book on paper folding and see what other surprises await you.

Materials:
- 5" square sheets of paper (this is a convenient size to use, but you may use any size as long as it is perfectly square)

1. Give each child a square sheet of paper. Help children locate the center of their papers by first folding the papers in half diagonally one way, opening the papers, and then folding them diagonally the other way. Open the papers. The exact center is where the two fold lines cross.
2. Fold all four corners of the paper to the center, being careful to align each point on the exact center mark.
3. Turn the paper over so that the folded corners are on the underside. Fold the new points to the center and crease firmly.
4. Turn the folded paper back over to the original side and once again fold the new corners in to the exact center. The square should now be 1¾" in size.
5. Open the paper and then repeat Step 2 above. Because of the creases made by the other folds, the paper will look like this:

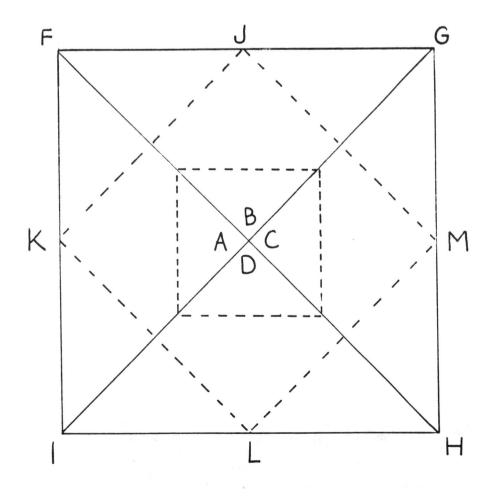

6. Squeeze M and L together to meet in the center so that point H sticks up. In the same way, bring point J and K to the center. The paper will look like this:

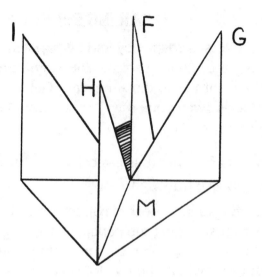

7. Take hold of points H and F and bend them back and down. This will fold the paper diagonally so that the paper will look like this:

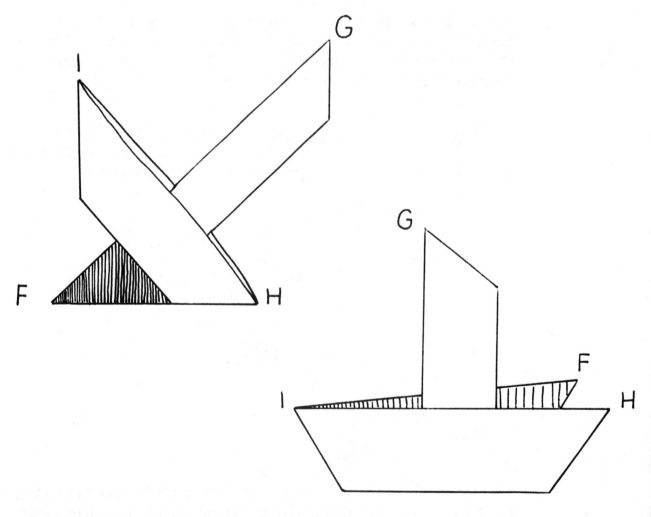

8. Turn point F back against point H to make a sailboat!

SKELETONS

All Souls' Day celebrations in Mexico and Central America are decorated with lots of skeletons (see page 24). There are numerous ways to make skeletons. Select one of the methods here.

Note: If, in your judgment, this activity may be disturbing to children or parents, you might choose not to use it.

Rolled Typing-Paper Skeleton

Materials:
- white typing paper
- ¼" dowel stick (15" long)
- string
- scissors
- paper-towel tube
- glue
- black marker
- 15" length of soft wire
- cellophane tape
- 6" x 9" index cards

1. Roll 4 sheets of typing paper the long way around a dowel stick to form skeleton legs. Roll 4 sheets of typing paper the short way around the dowel stick to make skeleton arms. Tape the edges of the rolls together.

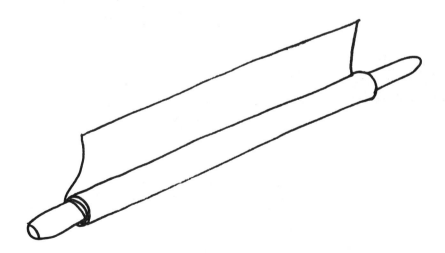

2. Cut 2 feet, 2 hands, and 2" half discs from index cards (see patterns on pages 134-135). Then help children draw and then cut out 2 skeleton heads from index cards.

3. Use a black marker to draw bones on the paper rolls, hands, feet, and discs.

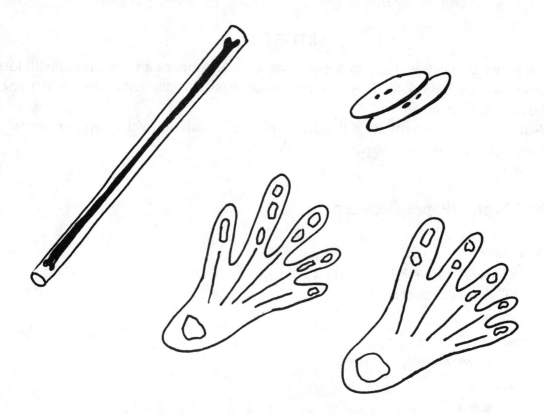

4. Tape a sheet of typing paper around a paper-towel tube.
5. Cut 4 sets of rib bones, 1 set of shoulder bones, and 1 set of pelvic bones from index cards (see patterns on pages 134-135).
6. Make a needle from the wire. Thread string through the "needle" and string the body parts together as shown here. Glue the head shapes on the string. Leave enough string at the top for hanging.

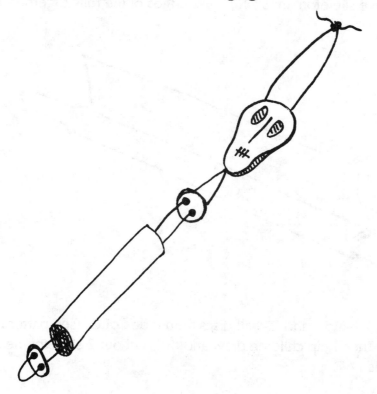

7. Glue the ribs, shoulder bones, and pelvic bones onto the paper-towel tube by placing one of each set of bones on either side of the tube and then gluing or taping the ends.

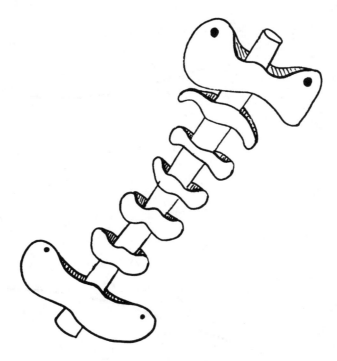

8. Punch holes at the bottoms of the shoulder and pelvic bones and feet as shown. Tie on the arm and leg tubes and hands and feet made in Steps 1 and 2.

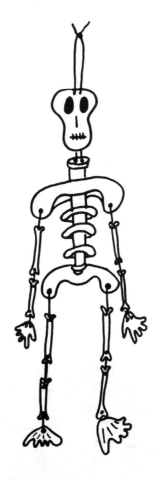

Skeleton Patterns

Skeleton Patterns

Coat-Hanger Skeleton Mobile

Materials:
- 13 coat hangers
- pliers
- tagboard
- scissors
- thread

1. Use a pliers to bend the coat hangers into the shapes of the parts of the body. Make a head, arm bones, leg bones, feet, hands, rib bones, shoulder bones, and a pelvic bone.

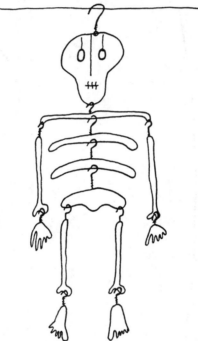

2. Cut a mouth and eyes out of tagboard. Suspend these parts by threads from the skull.
3. Hang the skeleton as a mobile in a doorway.

Paper-Tube/Paper-Plate Skeleton Mobile

Materials:
- paper plates
- paper-towel tubes
- string
- scissors

1. Cut out ribs, arm bones, leg bones, a head, hands, feet, and a pelvic bone from paper plates (see patterns on pages 134-135).
2. Use paper-towel tubes for the shoulder bone and spine.
3. Use a needle and string to attach the parts together.
4. Hang the skeleton from a doorway or from the ceiling in the classroom.

STICK HORSES

Horses were first introduced to the Americas by European settlers. Horses are an integral part of Mexico and Central America today. Stick horses are a favorite with Mexican and Central American children, just as they are with children all over the world. Invite children to make stick horses to "ride" in their Mexican and Central American celebrations!

Materials:
- 3' long 1" dowel stick (or an old broom handle) for each child
- wheat paste
- ½" newspaper strips
- masking tape
- grocery sacks
- tempera paint
- paintbrushes
- yarn

1. Give each child a dowel stick and a grocery sack. Invite children to stuff their grocery sacks with newspaper. Have children insert one end of their dowel sticks or broom handles into their sacks. Help children use masking tape to fasten the sacks to the sticks.

2. Encourage children to form the bags into horse-head shapes. Use masking tape to keep the bags in shape.

3. Invite children to apply strips of newspaper dipped in wheat paste in layers around the head shapes.

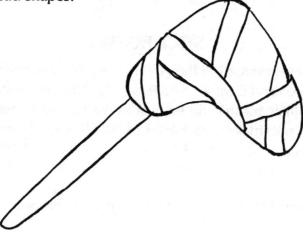

4. When the bases are firmly shaped, encourage children to add details, such as ears, eyebrows, nostrils, and mouth, with mash (see page 112) or wadded paper secured with papier-mâché strips.

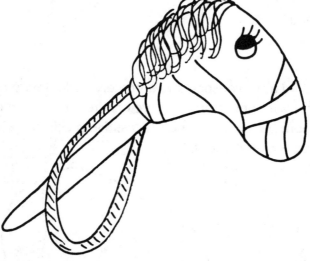

5. Let the horse heads dry for several days and then invite children to paint the heads and highlight the features. Then paint a coat of shellac over each entire head. Be sure the room is well ventilated when using shellac.

6. After the shellac is dry, help children glue on yarn manes. Add straps for reins, if the children wish.

TREE OF LIFE

A Mexican or Central American may make a tree of life to represent a new beginning. A tree of life is often made for Carnival (see page 52). In Mexico, a tree of life
is made from clay. Invite children to work together to make a large tree of life for the
classroom—a few children make the base and the others make the items to hang on
the branches. Create new shapes to hang on the tree for each season and fiesta.
Encourage children to make miniatures that enhance a theme being studied in
school.

Materials:
- large can
- tree branch (to fit in the can)
- 5 lbs self-hardening clay
- paper clips
- tin snips
- tempera paint
- paintbrushes
- plastic spray

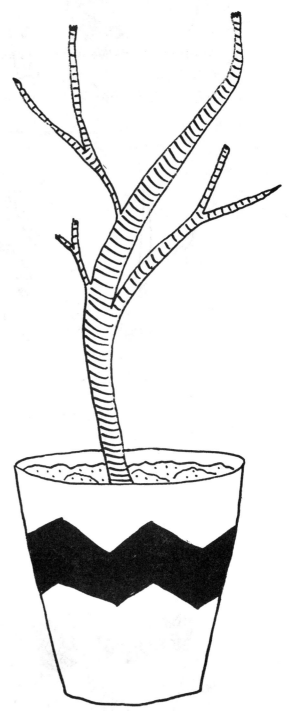

1. Put some clay in the bottom of a
   can and insert a tree branch.
2. Starting at the bottom, have children cover the tree branch with
   clay until it is evenly and gener-
   ously covered.
3. Invite the children to make little
   balls, flowers, leaves, bunnies, or
   other objects appropriate to hang
   on the tree for a particular fiesta or
   season.
4. Use tin snips to cut wire loops
   from paper clips. Insert the wire
   loops into the clay miniatures as
   hangers. Cover the wire with clay
   to make a stronger attachment.
   Set the miniatures aside. (Clay
   pieces that will remain a permanent part of the tree, such as
   leaves and flowers, should be
   glued on directly.)

5. Let the clay tree and miniatures dry thoroughly before painting. Then invite children to paint the tree and the miniatures.
6. Then carefully lay the tree down on a bed of paper towels and glue on the leaves, flowers, and other permanent miniatures children wish to include on the base. Let the glue dry completely.

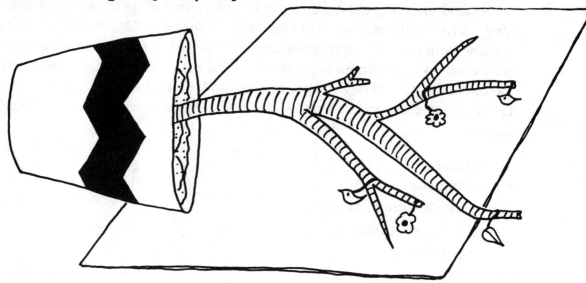

7. Invite children to touch up the paint in the places where they glued. Then spray the entire tree and miniatures with a plastic spray.
8. Encourage children to hang their miniatures on the tree.

TREE OF LIFE WALL HANGING

This tree of life idea comes from Metepec, an area very close to Mexico City. Encourage children to try creating imaginative plant and animal designs.

Materials:
- graph paper
- wax paper
- cookie sheet
- spatula
- baker's clay
- tempera paint
- paintbrushes
- plastic spray

1. Draw a tree base on a sheet of graph paper cut the size of a cookie sheet.

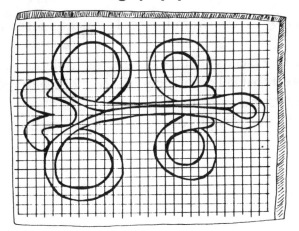

2. Prepare a batch of baker's clay (see Baker's Clay on page 82).
3. Roll out the dough to form long snakes.
4. Lay a sheet of wax paper over the graph-paper design to use as a working surface. Place the coils of dough on the wax paper and then have the children shape them along the lines of the tree pattern.

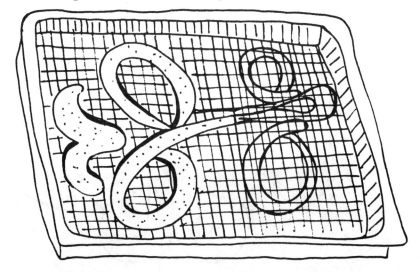

5. Invite children to use clay to make flowers, leaves, birds, or other plants and animals that they might use as decoration.

6. Carefully place the clay tree base and decorative pieces on a cookie sheet. Bake in a 275° F oven until hard—from 1 to 3 hours!

7. Before removing the tree from the cookie sheet, loosen it with a spatula while it is still hot.

8. When all the clay pieces are cool, encourage children to paint them in brilliant colors. Suggest that children apply one coat of white paint first as a primer. The colors will be much brighter.

9. Glue the decorative clay pieces on the tree and then spray the entire piece with a plastic spray.

WEAVINGS

Mexican and Central American weavings are colorful and often very complicated. Perhaps the most effective technique to make copies of complicated woven patterns is to use brightly colored yarns on burlap. This method can be as complicated as the imagination will allow. These weavings make wonderful placemats.

Materials:
  • burlap
  • yarn

1. Cut pieces of burlap to the size desired.
2. Pull out several threads that are adjacent to one another.

3. Gather several of the exposed threads and tie them together with yarn. Invite children to pull other groups of threads and see what kinds of patterns develop.

WEAVING ON A LOOM

Materials:
- sturdy cardboard (or pebbleboard)
- craft knife
- yarn
- scissors

1. Make cardboard (or pebbleboard) looms by using a craft knife to cut notches approximately ¾" deep and about every quarter inch along opposite ends of each piece of cardboard. It is best not to make this type of loom too large.
2. String yarn back and forth lengthwise across the looms.

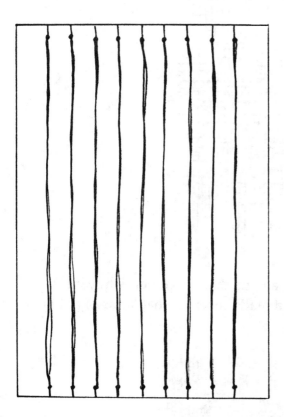 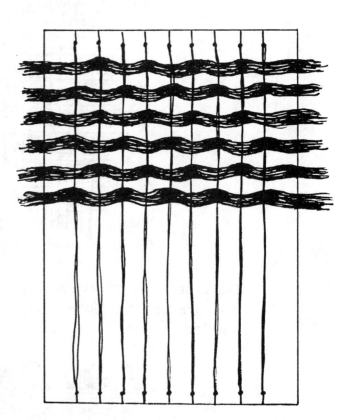

3. Invite children to weave lengths of yarn in and out of the lengthwise yarn from one side of the loom to the other. Help children try to keep the yarn straight at all times for a uniform-looking weave.
4. Encourage children to experiment with various patterns to make unique designs. For example, children might weave over two threads, then under three, and again over two and then under three, and so on. Variety may also be explored by using different colors of yarn to create stripes of color.

FOODS

There are many differences in food preparation from country to country and region to region throughout Mexico and Central America. Mexican cooking is probably the spiciest of all with many kinds of chiles—red, green, jalapeño, brown—all waiting to nip the unwary pallet.

Some foods prepared and enjoyed quite universally in Mexico and Central America are beans, rice, chicken, pork stew, tamales, and corn. Tropical fruits, such as papayas, mangos, pineapples, cherimoyas, and avocados, are also enjoyed.

Costa Rica has a very large European population and this is reflected in the foods eaten there. The other countries have various Indian-European background ratios. This has a great influence on foods of the culture.

Encourage parents and other friends to share Mexican and Central American foods and recipes with the children. Invite the children to assist with food preparation in the classroom as well. Savor the many different tastes of Mexico and Central America!

ALMENDRADO

(Almond Dessert)

The colors of this delicious dessert represent the red, white, and green Mexican flag. It's a favorite to serve for Independence Day! (See page 12.) A simple variation is to make this dessert with cherry and lime gelatin (for the red and green portions of the dessert) and whipped cream (for the white portion).

Have children wash their hands and the working surface area before handling the food items. Gather together the following ingredients and supplies.

Utensils:
sauce pan
mixing spoon
portable mixer
measuring spoons
measuring cups
hot plate or stove
clear glass serving bowl or mold
mixing bowls
plastic wrap (optional)
serving platter

Ingredients:
1 package unflavored gelatin
½ cup water
6 egg whites
½ cup sugar
1 tsp almond extract
red and green food coloring
¾ cup chopped almonds

1. Put gelatin and water in a saucepan. Stir over medium heat until the gelatin dissolves completely. Remove the saucepan from the heat and cool for 15 minutes.

2. Beat egg whites in a mixing bowl until they are frothy.

3. Continue beating the egg whites as you add sugar and the dissolved gelatin. Beat until the mixture forms stiff peaks. Gradually stir in the almond extract.

4. Divide the mixture evenly among 3 mixing bowls.

5. Tint the mixture in one bowl bright pink by adding a few drops of red food coloring. Color the mixture in another bowl bright green by adding a few drops of green food coloring. Mix almonds in the uncolored mixture in the third bowl. Be careful of any allergies to nuts in the classroom.

6. Spread the pink mixture evenly in a glass serving bowl or salad mold. Chill for ten minutes. Spread the white mixture on top, being careful not to disturb the pink layer. Chill 10 minutes before spreading the green mixture evenly on the very top.

7. Chill for at least 2 hours or until the layers set completely.

8. Cut around the sides of the bowl or mold with a knife and then place the bottom and sides of the bowl or mold in warm water for a few seconds to loosen the gelatin. Shake gently to test for looseness. Then place a serving platter over the bowl or mold and turn over. Gently remove the bowl or mold.

9. Spoon Natillas de Almendrado, a rich custard sauce, over each serving (recipe provided on page 147). Vanilla pudding may be substituted for an easy variation.

NATILLAS DE ALMENDRADO

Utensils:
double-boiler
mixing spoon
portable mixer
measuring spoons
measuring cups
hot plate or stove
serving bowl
mixing bowl
plastic wrap (optional)

Ingredients:
6 egg yolks
¼ cup sugar
⅛ tsp salt
2 cups hot milk
½ tsp almond extract

1. In a medium mixing bowl, beat egg yolks, sugar, and salt until well-blended.
2. Gradually add hot milk to the mixture, stirring constantly.
3. Pour water into the bottom pan of a double-boiler. Pour the hot milk and egg mixture into the top pan.
4. Cook and stir constantly over medium heat until the mixture coats a metal spoon (about 10 minutes).
5. Remove the pan from the heat and add almond extract. Cool the mixture and then refrigerate for at least 30 minutes. Makes about 3 cups.

SERVING SUGGESTION:
Have children make miniature paper flags of Mexico (see Independence Day on page 12). Place a ball of clay in the bottom of a colorful pot. Attach the flags to thin dowel sticks and then insert the sticks into the clay to make a festive centerpiece. Hang a banner above the table entitled "¡Viva la Mexico!" and enjoy the colorful dessert.

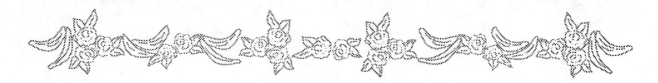

PAN DE MUERTO
(Bread of the Dead)

Don't let the name of this bread scare you! It is enjoyed during All Souls' Day, a special celebration on November 2 (see page 24). Families honor their departed relatives on this day by serving this special bread made in the shape of a skull and crossbones! Invite children to enjoy eating each delicious, crusty, brown piece as they celebrate All Souls' Day the Mexican and Central American way.

Note: If, in your judgment, this activity may be disturbing to children or parents, you might choose not to use it.

Have children wash their hands and the working surface area before handling the food items. Gather together the following ingredients and supplies.

Utensils:	Ingredients:
basting brush	frozen bread dough
wax paper	cooking oil
hot pads	1 egg white, slightly beaten
cookie sheet	colored sugar (optional)

1. Heat oven to 350° F.
2. Follow the directions provided on the package for thawing the frozen bread dough. Divide the thawed dough in half.
3. Grease a cookie sheet with cooking oil. Form half of the dough into a flattened ball to place on the cookie sheet.
4. Divide the other half of the dough into fourths. Roll two of the sections into 5" length ropes, about 1" thick. Flatten the ends to look like the rounded ends of bones. Arrange the ropes into an "X" on top of the large round ball of dough on the cookie sheet. Use egg white as glue.
5. Roll another section of the dough into a ball. Make a slight depression on top of the large bread loaf and then place this ball in the depression to make the "skull on the crossbones." Use egg white as glue.
6. Form 4 teardrops from the remaining section of dough. Use egg white to attach the drops to the sides of the large loaf.
7. Cover with wax paper and allow the dough to rise in a warm place for about ½ an hour.
8. Brush the unbaked bread with the remaining egg white before baking. You may wish to sprinkle colored sugar over the dough as well.
9. Bake for 30 minutes or until the raised design portions of the bread brown nicely, giving a rich look to the bread.
10. Carefully remove the bread from the oven.

ROSCA DE LOS REYES
(Kings' Bread)

This bread is traditionally served on January 6, Day of the Three Kings (see page 38). And what fun it is! A small porcelain doll or lima bean is baked in the bread and, according to the custom, the person who finds it must give a party on Candlemas Day, February 2 (see page 48). Have the children break open their pieces of bread to find the small doll or bean before eating it.

Have children wash their hands and the working surface area before handling the food items. Gather together the following ingredients and supplies.

Utensils:	Ingredients:
scissors	frozen bread dough
cookie sheet	flour
mixing spoons	2 Tbsp granulated sugar
measuring spoons	½ tsp cinnamon
measuring cups	½ cup chopped pecans
small mixing bowls	½ cup candied fruits
hot pads	½ cup powdered sugar
wax paper	¼ tsp vanilla
rack	milk

1. Heat oven to 350° F.
2. Follow the directions provided on the package for thawing the frozen bread dough. Divide the thawed dough in half.
3. On a floured surface, form the dough into a 9" x 15" rectangle.
4. In a small bowl, mix together the sugar and cinnamon.
5. Sprinkle the sugar mixture, nuts, and half of the candied fruits on the dough. Save some of the "jewels" (candied fruit and nuts) to top the "crown" after it is frosted.
6. Roll up the rectangle, beginning on the long side. Pinch the rolled edge to seal well.
7. Place the dough, sealed edge down, on a cookie sheet. Shape the dough into a ring and pinch the ends together. Make cuts in the ring of dough at even intervals with a scissors. "Hide" a little porcelain doll or lima bean in one of the dough sections.
8. Cover the dough with wax paper and allow to rise on a cookie sheet for ½ hour.
9. Bake for 30 minutes or until the top browns nicely, giving a rich look to the bread. Carefully remove the bread from the oven and cool on a rack.
10. Meanwhile, mix together in a small bowl the powdered sugar, vanilla, and milk to a spreading consistency. Dribble this mixture over the cooled loaf. Top the frosting with the remaining nuts and candied fruits to represent "jewels" on a "crown." Be careful of any allergies to nuts in the classroom.

CAMOTE
(Sweet Potato Candy)

Ask the children if they have ever heard of sweet potato candy. This unique sweet is served in Mexico on May 5 to celebrate Mexico's victory over the French in the Battle of Puebla (see page 68). Camote is made and sold in dozens of shops throughout Puebla.

Have the children wash their hands and the working surface area before handling the food items. Gather together the following ingredients and supplies.

Utensils:	Ingredients:
2 saucepans	1 20-oz can crushed pineapple
mixing spoons	1-lb can sweet potatoes
measuring spoons	4 cups sugar
measuring cups	powdered sugar
mixing bowl	
can opener	
hot plate or stove	
9" x 13" pan	
blender	

1. Open the can of pineapple and empty the contents into a saucepan.
2. Cook the pineapple over medium heat until it is tender (about 10 minutes).
3. Remove the pineapple from the heat and cool slightly. Put the pineapple in a blender and blend on high for a few seconds. Pour the mixture into a mixing bowl.
4. Open the can of sweet potatoes and puree the contents in a blender.
5. Pour the pureed sweet potatoes into a saucepan and heat thoroughly over medium heat (about 5 minutes). Stir in the sugar and simmer for 5 minutes.
6. Remove the mixture from the heat and cool slightly.
7. Add the sweet potato mixture to the pineapple and stir to mix. Pour the blended mixture into a 9" x 13" pan and allow to set for 24 to 36 hours.
8. When the mixture is firm enough to mold, divide the mixture into small portions and roll the portions into cigar-like shapes. Refrigerate. Roll the shapes in powdered sugar before serving.

CHICKEN TOSTADAS

Tostadas not only taste good and look good, but are easy to make as well! Begin with a corn tortilla and fill it with colorful vegetables, chicken, and cheese.

Have the children wash their hands and the working surface area before handling the food items. Gather together the following ingredients and supplies.

Utensils:
electric skillet
measuring spoons
measuring cups
spatula
hot pads
mixing bowl
mixing spoons
paper towels

Ingredients:
2 cups shredded lettuce
⅓ cup shredded carrot
2 Tbsp salad oil
1 Tbsp lemon juice
1 Tbsp vinegar
salsa or taco sauce
cooking oil
6 6-inch corn tortillas
1 10-½ oz can jalapeño bean dip
1 cup guacamole dip (see Guacamole on page 155)
2 cups cooked chicken (white meat), shredded
¾ cup shredded cheese
1 chopped tomato
⅓ cup sliced olives

1. Mix the shredded lettuce and carrots together in a medium bowl.
2. In another bowl, stir together the salad oil, lemon juice, and vinegar. Pour this mixture over the lettuce and carrots.
3. Mix the salsa (or taco sauce) and bean dip together in a small bowl and stir until the mixture is of spreading consistency.
4. Heat a small amount of cooking oil in a skillet and fry the tortillas over medium heat for about 30 seconds on each side, or until crisp. Drain the tortillas on paper towels. (Keep the fried tortillas warm in a 300° F oven.)
5. To serve, place a tortilla on each plate and layer the remaining ingredients in the following order: bean dip mixture, guacamole dip, chicken, lettuce mixture, cheese, tomato, and olives.

CORN CAKES

Corn cakes are a must at the yearly fiesta in the shrine of Our Lady of Guadalupe! (See page 30.) They are delicious served with honey. You don't have to travel to the shrine of Our Lady of Guadalupe to enjoy them. Try some!

Have the children wash their hands and the working surface area before handling the food items. Gather together the following ingredients and supplies.

Utensils:
comal (frying pan)
measuring spoons
measuring cups
hot plate or stove
spatula
hot pads
mixing bowl
mixing spoon
wax paper
paper towels
ribbons
colored tissue paper

Ingredients:
2 cups masa harina tortilla flour
1 cup milk
½ tsp salt
1 Tbsp sugar
1 tsp baking powder
cooking oil

1. In a medium bowl, mix together the masa harina and milk. Add salt, sugar, and baking powder to form a dough.
2. Place the dough on a sheet of wax paper. Divide the dough, making ¼" x 3" square cakes.
3. Heat a small amount of cooking oil in a comal. Fry the cakes lightly on both sides until they are brown.
4. Remove the corn cakes with a spatula and drain on paper towels.

SERVING SUGGESTION:
Stack the cooled corn cakes in piles of 6. Wrap each pile in colored tissue paper and tie with shredded ribbons.

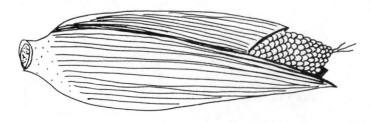

ENSALADA DE NOCHEBUENA
(Christmas Eve Salad)

This salad is a beautiful beginning course at midnight suppers on Christmas Eve in Mexico. It may be made with any available fruits. Be creative!

Have the children wash their hands and the working surface area before handling the food items. Gather together the following ingredients and supplies.

Utensils:
serving platter
mixing spoon
can opener
mixing bowl

Ingredients:
1 20-oz can pineapple chunks, drained (reserve juice)
1 can sliced beets, drained
2 large oranges, pared and sectioned
2 medium bananas, sliced
1 large apple, pared, cored, and sliced
lettuce leaves
½ cup peanuts

1. Prepare the fruits as listed in the ingredients.
2. Place the orange sections, banana slices, apple slices, and pineapple chunks in a bowl. Pour the reserved pineapple juice over the fruits and let stand for 10 minutes. Then drain.
3. Line a serving platter with lettuce leaves. Arrange the fruits on top in a colorful design.
4. Sprinkle peanuts over the top for a garnish. Be careful of any allergies to nuts in the classroom.

SERVING SUGGESTION:
Drizzle thinned mayonnaise over the salad just before serving.

GORDITAS
(Plump Tortillas)

These plump tortillas are delicious when topped with guacamole. They are a nutritious snack that will fill children up in a hurry. Make a large batch to put in the freezer and then pop some in the toaster to thaw whenever children need a quick snack!

Have children wash their hands and the working surface area before handling the food items. Gather together the following ingredients and supplies.

Utensils:
blender
electric skillet
mixing spoon
measuring spoons
measuring cups
hot pads
mixing bowl
paper towels
can opener

Ingredients:
8-oz can red kidney beans
½ tsp crushed red pepper
1 cup water
¾ tsp salt
1¾ cups masa harina tortilla flour
½ tsp baking powder
cooking oil

1. Open the can of kidney beans and empty the contents into a blender. Add pepper, water, and salt and blend until the mixture becomes smooth.

2. In a mixing bowl, combine masa harina and baking powder. Add the bean mixture and mix well to form a dough. Cover the mixture and let stand for 15 minutes.

3. Divide the dough into 24 parts. Flatten each part into a 2" circle.

4. Heat ⅛" cooking oil in an electric skillet. Fry the flattened dough about 1½ minutes on each side, or until crisp. Remove and drain the gorditas on paper towels.

SERVING SUGGESTION:
   Top with a dollop of guacamole (see Guacamole on page 155) and a radish slice. Makes 24 servings.

GUACAMOLE
(Avocado Sauce)

Historians believe that guacamole was served centuries ago by the Aztec in Mexico. The recipe has changed little over the years. Connect with these ancient people and make and enjoy some guacamole!

Have the children wash their hands and the working surface area before handling the food items. Gather together the following ingredients and supplies.

Utensils:
blender
serving dish
mixing spoon
measuring spoons
knife
garlic press
cutting board

Ingredients:
2 medium avocados
½ small onion
1 clove garlic
2 Tbsp lemon juice
½ tsp salt
¼ tsp pepper

1. Peel the avocados. Cut them open, remove the seeds (save the seeds to plant), and then cut the avocados into small pieces.
2. Peel and dice the onion.
3. Mince one clove of garlic in a garlic press.
4. Place the diced avocados, minced onions, garlic, lemon juice, salt, and pepper into a blender. Cover and blend until the ingredients are well-mixed.
5. Pour the mixture into a serving dish. Makes 1¼ cups.
6. Place an avocado seed in the guacamole until ready to serve. The seed will help keep the guacamole green.

SERVING SUGGESTION:
Use as a dip for chips or as a sauce to serve with Mexican dishes.

HORCHATA
(Spanish Drink)

Horchata is especially popular in Central America! This drink was first brought to Mexico and Central America from Spain. It was originally made by soaking and grinding raw rice and almonds. This recipe is a refreshing modern-day version of the original. You may make it with other fruits besides cantaloupe.

Have the children wash their hands and the working surface area before handling the food items. Gather together the following ingredients and supplies.

Utensils:
knife
large spoon
blender
measuring spoons
measuring cups
large pitcher
cutting board
strainer

Ingredients:
cantaloupe
1 cup cold water
1½ Tbsp granulated sugar
1½ tsp lime juice or to taste

1. Cut the cantaloupe into fourths. Scoop out the seeds and remove the rind. Then cut the cantaloupe into bite-size pieces.
2. Put the cantaloupe pieces and the remaining ingredients in a blender and blend for 5 minutes. Refrigerate for 5 hours.
3. Strain into a pitcher and serve.

SERVING SUGGESTION:
    Serve over ice.

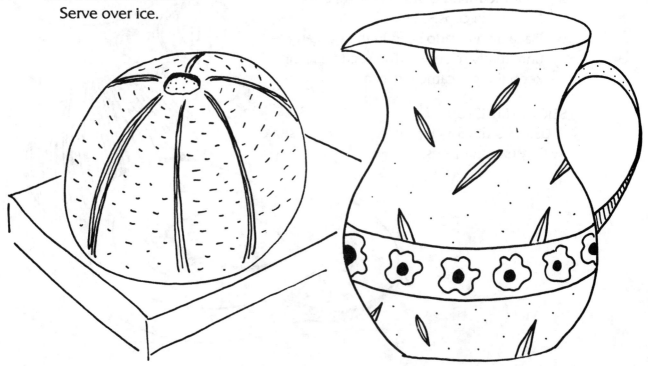

MEXICAN BANANA BAKE

If plantains are available in a supermarket near you, buy some to try in this recipe. Plantains grow in Mexico and Central America. They look like large bananas, but are less sweet and need to be cooked before eating. Let the plantains ripen until the skin is black and the fruit inside is soft before using. It's fun to try new foods!

Have the children wash their hands and the working surface area before handling the food items. Gather together the following ingredients and supplies.

Utensils:
blender
mixing spoon
knife
1 quart casserole

Ingredients:
1 3-oz package cream cheese, softened
¼ cup packed brown sugar
¼ cup half-and-half
⅛ tsp ground cinnamon
5 medium bananas (or plantains)
1 Tbsp margarine

1. Preheat oven to 325° F.
2. Place the cream cheese, brown sugar, half-and-half, and cinnamon in a blender. Cover and blend on high for about 30 seconds, or until the mixture is smooth.
3. Slice half of the bananas into a greased 1-quart casserole. Dot with margarine.
4. Spread half of the cream cheese mixture over the bananas.
5. Repeat with another layer of sliced bananas and top with the remaining cream cheese mixture.
6. Bake uncovered 20 to 25 minutes, or until the contents are hot and bubbly.

MEXICAN HOT CHOCOLATE

Traditionally, Mexican hot chocolate is made of chocolate blended with sugar, cinnamon and, occasionally, ground almonds. Mexicans make it frothy by beating it with a special carved, wooden beater called a *molinillo*. You may get similar results with a portable mixer.

Have the children wash their hands and the working surface area before handling the food items. Gather together the following ingredients and supplies.

Utensils:
large saucepan
mixing spoon
measuring cups
measuring spoons
hot pads
portable mixer

Ingredients:
½ cup sugar
3 oz unsweetened chocolate
1 tsp cinnamon
6 cups milk
2 beaten eggs
2 tsp vanilla

1. In a large saucepan, cook and stir the sugar, chocolate, cinnamon, and 1 cup milk over medium heat until the chocolate melts. Then stir in the remaining milk.
2. Mix 1 cup of the hot mixture with the beaten eggs, stirring constantly. Quickly stir the mixture into the saucepan. Heat for 2 minutes over low heat.
3. Use hot pads to remove the pan from the heat. Add vanilla and then beat the hot mixture with a portable mixer until the chocolate is frothy.

SERVING SUGGESTION:
Serve the chocolate hot in mugs topped with whipped cream and sticks of cinnamon.

POLVORONES
(Mexican Wedding Cakes)

Polvorones are special cookies that may be enjoyed at any Mexican or Central American fiesta.

Have the children wash their hands and the working surface area before handling the food items. Gather together the following ingredients and supplies.

Utensils:
mixing bowl
mixing spoon
measuring cups
measuring spoons
hot pads
spatula
cookie sheet

Ingredients:
1 cup margarine, softened
½ cup powdered sugar
1 tsp vanilla
2 cups flour
⅛ tsp salt
½ cup chopped pecans
powdered sugar

1. Preheat oven to 350° F.
2. Use a portable mixer to cream the margarine, powdered sugar, and vanilla in a large mixing bowl.
3. Gradually add the flour, salt, and pecans and beat until the dough is well-blended. Be careful of any allergies to nuts in the classroom.
4. Chill the dough for a ½ hour.
5. Roll the dough into 1" balls. Place the balls on a cookie sheet and bake for 20 minutes.
6. Use hot pads to carefully remove the cookie sheet from the oven. Use a spatula to remove the hot cookies.
7. Pour some powdered sugar into a small bowl and roll the hot cookies in the powdered sugar until thoroughly coated. Cool the cookies and then roll them in the powdered sugar once again.

SERVING SUGGESTION:

Polvorones may be wrapped in tissue paper by rolling the cookie in the paper, bunching the ends of the paper, and twisting the ends. Fringe the ends of the tissue paper to give the wrapped cookies a festive look.

PUPUSAS

Pupusas, a favorite treat from Honduras and El Salvador, are served for Day of Our Lady of Guadalupe fiestas (see page 30). But they are delicious to make and eat anytime!

Have the children wash their hands and the working surface area before handling the food items. Gather together the following ingredients and supplies.

Utensils:
comal (electric skillet)
mixing spoon
measuring cups
hot pads
spatula
mixing bowl
cooking oil

Ingredients:
2 cups masa harina tortilla flour
1½ cups water
½ lb cheese (cheddar, jack, or farmer cheese)
bacon bits

1. Mix masa harina and water together in a large mixing bowl.
2. Form the dough into a ball. Then divide the ball in half.
3. Put bacon bits and a slice of cheese in the middle of each ball of dough.
4. Pat the balls into cakes approximately 4" x ¾" thick.
5. Fry the cakes in a lightly greased comal on medium heat. Cook slowly for about 3 minutes on each side. Use a spatula to remove the hot cakes.

OIL

SALSA PICANTE

(Hot Sauce)

Some like this sauce hot, others like it mild. But no matter how you like it, salsa picante is a must for many Mexican dishes. It's delicious as a dip for tortilla chips. Invite children to try some!

Have the children wash their hands and the working surface area before handling the food items. Gather together the following ingredients and supplies.

Utensils:
saucepan
mixing spoon
blender
measuring spoons
knife
cutting board
hot plate or stove
garlic press

Ingredients:
½ can pickled jalapeño chiles (optional)
2 fresh, unpeeled tomatoes
¼ chopped onion
3 cloves of garlic
1 tsp vegetable oil
¼ tsp oregano
¼ tsp salt

1. Chop the chiles finely (optional) and dice the tomatoes and onion (you may use a food processor to chop the onion and the chiles, but not the tomatoes because they may get too mushy). Mince the garlic in a garlic press.

2. Place the diced tomatoes, onion, chiles, and minced garlic (including the juices) in a blender and blend on high speed until pureed.

3. Heat the oil in a saucepan and then add the tomato mixture, oregano, and salt. Bring the mixture to a boil. Reduce heat and simmer over low heat for about 10 minutes.

4. Use hot pads to remove the saucepan from the heat. Put the pan in a safe place to cool for 2 hours. This recipe makes about ¾ cup of sauce.

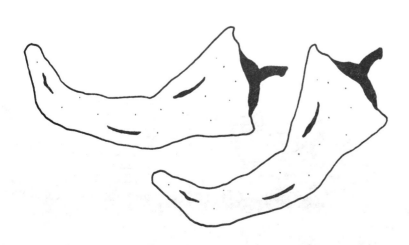

SOPA SECA DE TORTILLA

(Tortilla Casserole)

This is a "dry soup" enjoyed throughout Mexico and Central America. Other soups may be made from rice, noodles, or bread. Serve with meat, vegetables, or pasta.

Have the children wash their hands and the working surface area before handling the food items. Gather together the following ingredients and supplies.

Utensils:
electric skillet
mixing spoon
casserole dish
measuring spoons
measuring cups
hot pads
paper towels
knife

Ingredients:
10 6-inch tortillas
cooking oil
2 green bell peppers, cut in strips
1 medium onion, chopped (½ cup)
1 clove garlic, minced
1 tsp salt
1 cup whipping cream
1 cup shredded Monterey Jack cheese (4 oz)

1. Preheat oven to 350° F.
2. Slice tortillas into ½" x 3" strips.
3. Heat a small amount of cooking oil in an electric skillet. Fry a few tortilla strips at a time until they are limp (about 10 seconds). Drain the tortilla strips on paper towels.
4. Add green pepper strips, onion, and garlic to the oil. Cook until the onion is tender. Salt lightly.
5. In a casserole dish, mix together the tortilla strips, vegetables, whipping cream, and half the cheese. Cover and bake for 20 minutes.
6. Use hot pads to remove the casserole from the oven. Uncover and sprinkle the remaining cheese over the top. Return the casserole to the oven and bake uncovered for an additional 10 minutes.

SPOON BREAD

Corn tortillas are the national bread of Mexico, but there are many more breads to enjoy as well. Corn forms the basis for spoon bread and, as the name suggests, it is eaten with a spoon. Invite children to dig in!

Have the children wash their hands and the working surface area before handling the food items. Gather together the following ingredients and supplies.

Utensils:
mixing bowls
mixing spoon
measuring cups
measuring spoons
hot pads
9" x 13" pan

Ingredients:
1 can cream-style corn
¾ cup milk
⅓ cup melted margarine
2 eggs, slightly beaten
1 medium onion, chopped
1 cup cornmeal
½ tsp baking soda
½ tsp salt
4 jalapeño chiles, chopped (optional)
2 cups shredded cheddar cheese

1. Preheat oven to 350° F.
2. In a mixing bowl, stir together creamed corn, milk, melted margarine, eggs, and onion.
3. In a smaller bowl, mix together the dry ingredients—cornmeal, baking soda, and salt.
4. Add the dry mixture to the creamed corn mixture and stir until well mixed.
5. Grease a 9" x 13" pan with cooking oil. Pour half of the mixture into the pan.
6. Sprinkle 1 cup cheese and the chopped jalapeño chiles (if desired) on top.
7. Pour the remaining mixture over the cheese. Top with the remainder of the cheese. Bake for 45 minutes.
8. Use hot pads to remove the pan from the oven.

TACO PLATTER

This colorful platter is a delicious dip for tortilla chips—and it's easy to make. Enjoy it often.

Have the children wash their hands and the working surface area before handling the food items. Gather together the following ingredients and supplies.

Utensils:
serving platter
mixing spoon
measuring cups
measuring spoons
mixing bowl
knife
blender

Ingredients:
2 cans bean dip (10-oz size)
4 or 5 avocados
2 Tbsp lemon juice
¼ tsp salt and pepper
1 cup sour cream
½ cup mayonnaise
1 pkg taco seasoning
1 cup chopped green onion
1 can chopped ripe olives
2 cups chopped, seeded tomatoes
1 cup grated cheddar cheese

1. Spread the bean dip evenly on a serving platter.
2. Peel the avocados and remove the seeds. (Don't discard them—plant them!) Cut the avocados into small pieces and then put them into a blender. Add lemon juice, salt, and pepper. Cover and blend on high speed until smooth.
3. Spread the mixture evenly over the bean dip layer.
4. In a small bowl, mix together the sour cream, mayonnaise, and taco seasoning. Carefully spread this layer over the avocado layer.
5. Sprinkle chopped green onions, ripe olives, tomatoes, and cheddar cheese over the top layer on the platter.

MUSIC

Music has been called "the universal language." The music of Mexico and Central America is colorful and inviting with its strong rhythmic beat. Mexican and Central American music blends the music of Native Americans living in Central America before the arrival of Columbus, the music the Spanish brought from Europe, and the music of slaves brought from Africa to work in the mines and on the plantations in Mexico and Central America.

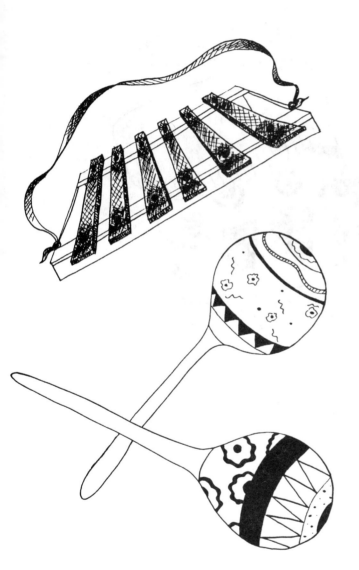

Music is heard everywhere in Mexico and Central America—at markets, concert halls, family fiestas, and certainly at all national holiday celebrations. It is truly an art as much as a folk music, combining the old and the new.

Incan, Mayan, and Aztec Native Americans created music that told stories of their gods and historical events. Some of these ancient chants are still heard today in parts of Mexico and Central America. Through some of their artwork, we know that drums, bells, bone scrapers, and shakers were popular instruments. The marimba was the most sophisticated instrument. Stringed instruments are a product of the Europeans.

Percussion instruments are used often in Mexican and Central American music. The emphasis on musical instruments is particularly strong in Nicaragua. Although the authentic instruments are probably difficult to find and show the children, facsimiles may be made and used in some of your classroom Mexican and Central American festivals.

Use the songs and musical instruments in this section to invite your children into the rhythmic beat of Mexico and Central America. Enjoy!

Note: Each song in this section is presented in both English and Spanish. Please note that the songs in English are not literal translations of the songs in Spanish, but the integrity of the Spanish lyrics is carefully maintained throughout.

Included as a companion to this resource is a cassette tape of the 17 songs in this music section. Side one of the tape offers the musical arrangements. Side two provides Spanish vocals, plus the music.

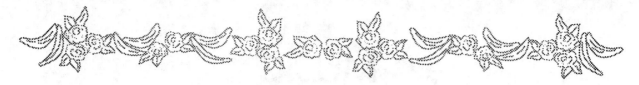

BONGO DRUMS

Bongo drums are often called "Drums of Joy." They were used to accompany a song by that title (see "El Tambor de la Alegría" on pages 209-212). The drum song was sung and danced at Native American festivals in Panama long ago. Invite children to make similar drums to accompany the songs. Children can play the drums by beating on them with their hands.

Materials:
- ice-cream cartons, empty and clean
- inner-tubing
- knife
- electrical tape
- tempera paint
- paintbrush
- feathers and scrap materials

1. Cut and stretch a sheet of inner-tubing to fit over the end of each ice-cream carton.
2. Tape the inner-tubing securely to the cartons with electrical tape.
3. Invite children to paint colorful designs and pictures on the sides of the drums. Decorate the painted drums as desired with scrap materials as well.

HAND DRUMS

In Nicaragua, there is an emphasis on musical instruments, particularly among children. Although the authentic instruments are difficult to make, facsimiles, such as these hand drums, may be produced and played for festival celebrations.

Materials:
- 2 sets of large embroidery hoops (for each drum)
- sheets of railroad board (picture matting)
- butcher paper
- masking tape
- scissors
- glue
- tempera paint
- paintbrush
- feathers, beads, and other decorative materials

1. Cut a piece of railroad board the same length as the circumference of the embroidery hoops.
2. Form a circle with the railroad board. Tape the seam securely with masking tape.
3. Glue the bottom half of an embroidery hoop around each end of the rolled railroad board.
4. Cut butcher paper to fit over the ends of the drums. Then soak the papers in liquid starch and stretch over the hoops at each end of the drums. These will serve as the drum heads.
5. Place the top hoops over the butcher paper and tighten. Trim off the excess butcher paper and then allow the drum heads to dry.
6. Invite children to paint colorful designs and pictures on the sides of the drums. Children may also wish to glue feathers and other decorative materials on the drums.

MARACAS

Maracas are dried gourds used as rattles. The dried seeds inside rattle when the gourds are shaken. Maracas are common rhythm instruments enjoyed and played during Mexican and Central American fiestas and parties or as integral parts of every-day music. You may make replicas of maracas using a variety of materials. Try making several and compare the sounds each produces.

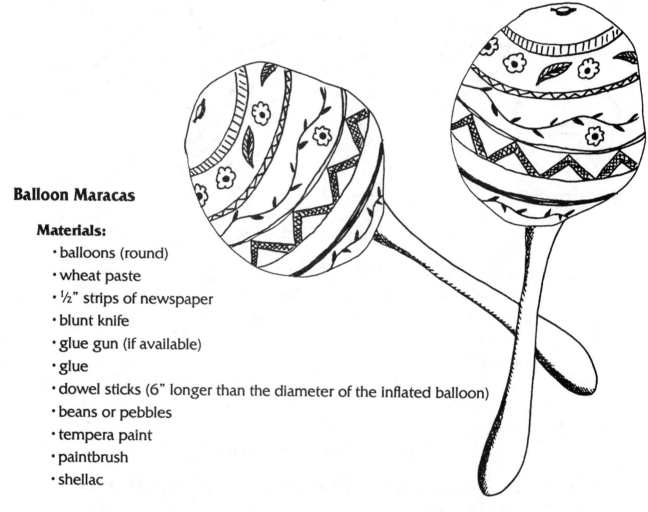

Balloon Maracas

Materials:

- balloons (round)
- wheat paste
- ½" strips of newspaper
- blunt knife
- glue gun (if available)
- glue
- dowel sticks (6" longer than the diameter of the inflated balloon)
- beans or pebbles
- tempera paint
- paintbrush
- shellac

1. Inflate and tie the balloons. Then invite children to cover the surfaces entirely with three to four layers of papier-mâché strips. Allow to dry. (This may take several days.)
2. Cut a small hole in the papier-mâché forms and remove the balloons inside.
3. Place approximately one dozen beans or pebbles in the opening of the maracas and then papier-mâché over the holes.
4. Help children put a dab of glue on the end of a dowel stick and insert it in one end of the shell all the way through until it sticks to the inside wall of the opposite side of each maraca. (Use a glue gun, if possible.)
5. Place glue around the handles where they enter the shells.
6. Invite children to paint the maracas in bright colors. After the paint dries, add a coat of shellac. Be sure the room is well ventilated when using shellac.

Box Maracas

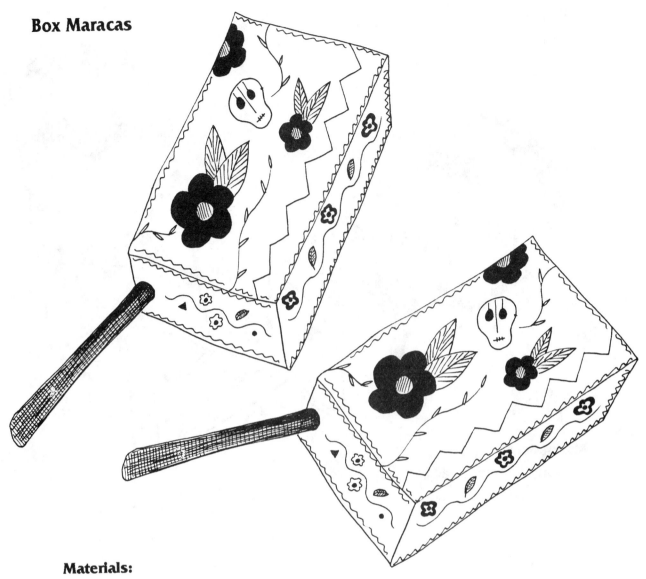

Materials:

- small cardboard boxes
- construction paper, tissue paper, or other colored papers
- dowel sticks (6" longer than the box)
- beans or pebbles
- glue
- hot-glue gun
- markers
- scrap materials

1. Help each child cut a small hole in the center of one edge of a small cardboard box.
2. Invite children to drop pebbles or beans into their boxes through the opening.
3. Dab glue on the end of the dowel sticks (if possible, use a glue gun) and insert through the holes and all the way through to the far inside wall of the opposite side.
4. Glue around the handles where they enter the boxes.
5. Encourage children to glue colored paper on the boxes and then use markers and scrap materials to decorate the boxes in holiday colors and designs.

Can Maracas

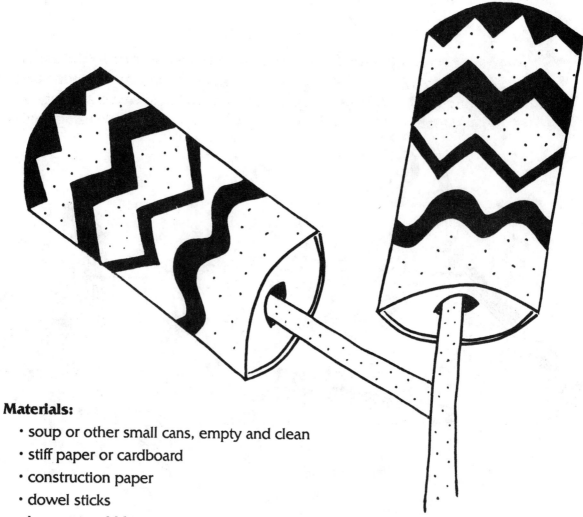

Materials:

- soup or other small cans, empty and clean
- stiff paper or cardboard
- construction paper
- dowel sticks
- beans or pebbles
- glue
- hot-glue gun
- markers
- scissors
- scrap materials

1. Cut circles from stiff paper or cardboard to fit over the open ends of the cans.
2. Invite children to put pebbles or beans inside the cans.
3. Dab glue on one end of the dowel sticks (use a hot-glue gun, if possible) and then insert the sticks, glue end first, through the holes all the way to the opposite ends of the cans.
4. Cut a small hole in the center of each paper circle and slip the circles onto the dowel sticks. Slide the circles down to the cans and then glue the circles to the open ends of the cans.
5. Put glue around the handles where they enter the cans.
6. Encourage children to cut colored paper to glue on the cans. Use markers and scrap materials for decoration.

MARIMBA

A marimba is one of the most sophisticated instruments made by the ancient Aztec, Mayan, and Inca tribes. Marimbas are generally made from wooden bars with hollowed-out gourds of different sizes hung from each bar to create a variety of tones, much like a xylophone. The following marimba can be made using bottles.

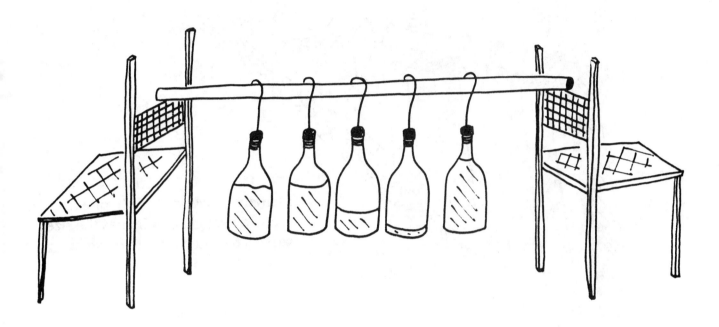

Materials:
- 8 or 10 bottles the same shape and size
- 8' stick (2" x 2" in diameter)
- string
- 2 chairs
- water
- spoons

1. Balance a pole or stick between the backs of two chairs. Tie the pole or stick to the chairs, if necessary.
2. Tie a string on each bottle and then suspend the bottles from the pole.
3. Have children fill the bottles with varying amounts of water—from full to empty—to give each bottle a different pitch when tapped with spoons or sticks. Try making an 8-note scale.

PARAGUAYAN HARP

Though Paraguay is part of South America, it is also considered part of Mexico and Central America. Paraguayan harps were played by gauchos (cowboys) for celebrations or just for relaxation. The harps are small enough to be held in the lap as they are played. Generally the harp has many strings, but the strings on these replicas are limited to the number of strings the frames will hold.

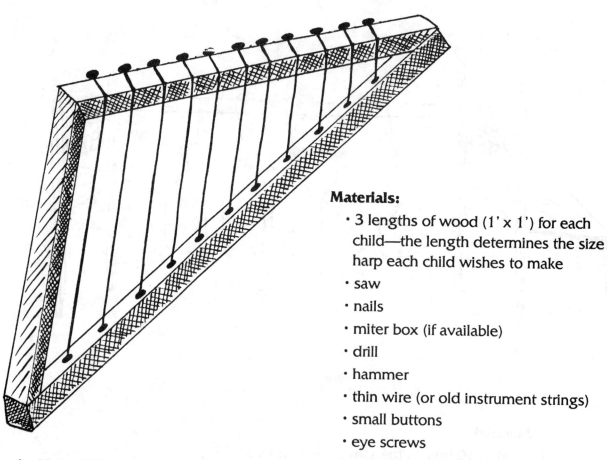

Materials:
- 3 lengths of wood (1' x 1') for each child—the length determines the size harp each child wishes to make
- saw
- nails
- miter box (if available)
- drill
- hammer
- thin wire (or old instrument strings)
- small buttons
- eye screws

1. Help children make triangular frames with three lengths of wood. First, nail two sides together at a right angle. Use a miter box, if possible. Position the third piece of wood in place and mark the sawing angles. Saw along the mark lines.

2. Drill small holes, about 1½" apart, along the inside edge of the third side and then nail the final piece of wood to the ends of the other sides.

3. Attach one end of each wire string to small buttons. Thread the other ends of the wires through the holes in side three of the harp, pulling the wires through the holes to the top side. Pull straight and mark the places on the top side where they touch.

4. Attach the free end of the wire strings to eye screws (wrap or wind them around the screw heads) and then screw in place next to the marks on the top side.

5. Tune the harps by turning the eye screws until the strings are tight. The longest strings will make the lowest sounds.

A la Víbora
The Serpent

A la
ví- bor- a de la mar, por a- quí pue- den pa- sar. Los de a- de-
lan - te cor - ren mu - cho, los de a - trás se que- da- rán.

The Serpent
A la Víbora

Like the ser - pent of the sea, a pass - age you must find, those in front must all run quick - ly, those in back are left be - hind.

Piñon, Pirulín

Spanish

1. Pi - ñon, pi - ñon, pi - ñon, pi - ru - lín, pi - ru - lín pi - ru - le - ro. Pi - ñon, pi - ñon, pi - ñon, pi - ru - lín, pi - ru - lín, pi - ru - lón.

2. Mi - guel, Mi - guel, Mi - guel, que la vuel - ta es - tá a la de - re - cha. Mi - guel, Mi - guel, Mi - guel, que la vuel - ta es - tá al re - vés.

3. Pi - ñon, pi - ñon, pi - ñon, tro - le, tro - le, tro - le - ro. Mi - guel, Mi - guel, Mi - guel, tro - le, tro - le, tro - le.

Piñon, Pirulín

English

1. Pi - ñon, pi - ñon, pi - ñon, pi - ru - lín, pi - ru - lín pi - ru - le - ro. Pi - ñon, pi - ñon, pi - ñon, pi - ru - lín, pi - ru - lín, pi - ru - lón.
2. Mi - guel, Mi - guel, Mi - guel, make a turn, make a turn to the right side. Mi - guel, Mi - guel, Mi - guel, make a turn, make a turn to the left.
3. Pi - ñon, pi - ñon, pi - ñon, tro - le, tro - le, tro - le - ro. Mi - guel, Mi - guel, Mi - guel, tro - le, tro - le, tro - le.

Charrada
Dance of the Mexican Horsemen

1. Ya des-can-sa el bur-ri-to de to-dos sus la-bor-es.
2. A-dios, a-dios, Pe-ri-co. Fiel y fuer-te e-ra. Lle-
3. To-dos le e-cha-rán de me-nos, no lo oi-rán re-buz-nar.

Dance of the Mexican Horsemen

Charrada

1. Oh now the lit - tle don - key rests from all his la - bors.
2. A - dios, a - dios, Pe - ri - co. Strong he all was and faith - ful.
3. Now all the folks will miss him. Hear no more his bray - ing.

He has gone to heav - en. Is mourned by all the neigh - bors. Tu
Car - ried all his bur - dens with kicks and glan - ces bale - ful. Tu
Loud the bell is toll - ing and all his friends are say - ing. Tu

ru - ru - ru - ru - ru. Tu ru - ru - ru - ru - ru. Tu
ru - ru - ru - ru - ru. Tu ru - ru - ru - ru - ru. Tu
ru - ru - ru - ru - ru. Tu ru - ru - ru - ru - ru. Tu

ru - ru - ru - ru - ru. Tu ru - ru - ru - ru - ru.
ru - ru - ru - ru - ru. Tu ru - ru - ru - ru - ru.
ru - ru - ru - ru - ru. Tu ru - ru - ru - ru - ru.

Fiesta! Mexico and Central America © 1993 Fearon Teacher Aids

Las Mañanitas
The Morning Song

Es - tas son las ma - ña - ni - tas que can -

ta - ba el rey Da - vid. A las mu - cha - chas bo - ni - tas se las can -

Fiesta! Mexico and Central America © 1993 Fearon Teacher Aids

The Morning Song
Las Mañanitas

We will sing a morn-ing greet - ing as king Da - vid used to do. He would sing it to the la - dies, and we will

Fiesta! Mexico and Central America © 1993 Fearon Teacher Aids

Fiesta! Mexico and Central America © 1993 Fearon Teacher Aids

El Coyotillo
Little Coyote

De las co-li-nas hay un au-lli-do, owoo, owoo, owoo, owoo.

Y do-lo-ri-do es. Ai, ai, ai, ai, ai.

Little Coyote
El Coyotillo

From out of the hills a cry sounds uy, uy, uy, uy.

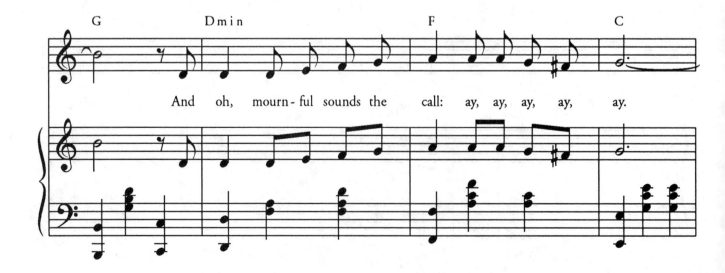

And oh, mourn-ful sounds the call: ay, ay, ay, ay, ay.

Fiesta! Mexico and Central America © 1993 Fearon Teacher Aids

Fiesta! Mexico and Central America © 1993 Fearon Teacher Aids

Feliz Cumpleaños
Happy Birthday

Happy Birthday
Feliz Cumpleaños

A Mambrú Chato

Pugnosed Mambrú

1. A Mam-brú cha-
2. Yo quie-ro un

to, ma-ta-ri-le, ri-le, ri-le, ¿Qué-que-rí-a, us-
pa-je, ma-ta-ri-le, ri-le, ri-le, Es-co-ja us-

ted? ma-ta-ri-le, ri-le, ron. 3. Yo es-co-jo a Pe-pe-i-llo, ma-ta-
ted, ma-ta-ri-le, ri-le, ron. 4. Le pon-dre-mos car-pin-te-ro, ma-ta-

ri - le, ri - le, ri - le. ¿Qué o - fi - cio le pon - dre - mos? ma - ta - ri - le, ri - le
ri - le, ri - le, ri - le. Es - e o - fi - cio sí le gus - ta, ma - ta - ri - le, ri - le

ron. 5. ¡Ce - le - bre - mos to - dos jun - tos, to - dos jun - tos la reu - nión,
ron. 6. Que el dí - a de tu san - to, se ce - le - bra la fun - ción!

Pugnosed Mambrú
A Mambrú Chato

1. Oh Mam- brú, Mam- brú, ma- ta- ri- le, ri- le, ri- le. Tell us what you want, ma- ta- ri- le, ri- le, ron. 3. I choose Jo- ey for my page, ma- ta-

2. I would like a page, ma- ta- ri- le, ri- le, ri- le. You must choose a page, ma- ta- ri- le, ri- le, ron. 4. It's a car- pen- ter he'll be, ma- ta-

ri - le, ri - le, ri - le. What will Jo - ey's job be? Ma - ta - ri - le, ri - le
ri - le, ri - le, ri - le. Jo - ey likes that job. Ma - ta - ri - le, ri - le

ron. 5. We are all here to - ge - ther with a spe - cial job to do.
ron. 6. We must ce - le - brate your birth - day. Hap - py Birth - day to you!

Tengo Una Muñeca

I Have a Doll

1. Ten-go u-na mu-ñe-ca ves-ti-da de a-zul,
2. La sa-qué a pa-se-o, se me en-fer-mó:

con su ca-mi-si-ta y su ca-ne-sú.
la me-tí en la ca-ma con mu-cho do-lor.

3. Es-ta ma-ña-ni-ta me di-jó el doc-tor,
4. Dos y dos son cua-tro, cua-tro y dos son seis:
5. Y o-cho, vien-ti-cua-tro, y o-cho, trein-ta y dos;

que le de ja - ra - be con el te - ne - dor.
seis y dos son o - cho, y o - cho, diez y seis:
la me - da - lla de o - ro me la lle - vo yo.

I Have a Doll
Tengo Una Muñeca

use a fork to give my doll her me - di - cine.

4. One and one make two, two and two make four,
5. Twen- ty - four means add - ing eight and thir - ty - two the same.

four and four are eight and six - teen is eight more.
I win the gold me - dal and I win the game!

Fiesta! Mexico and Central America © 1993 Fearon Teacher Aids

Los Pollitos

The Little Chicks

1. Los po-lli-tos di-cen: pí - o, pí - o pí - o,
2. La ga-lli-na bus-ca el ma-íz y el tri - go,
3. Ba-jo sus dos a - las, a-cu-rru-ca-di - tos,

cuan - do tie-nen ham-bre, cuan - do tie - nen frí - o.
les da la co-mi-da, y les pres-ta a-bri - go.
has - ta el o - tro dí - a, duer - men los po - lli - tos.

The Little Chicks
Los Pollitos

1. Lit - tle chicks are call - ing, pí - o, pí - o pí - o,
2. Mo - ther hen goes look - ing for grains of wheat and corn to
3. All a - round their mo - ther the chicks are snug - gled near. Be -

when they need to eat, or when they're feel - ing cold.
feed them for their din - ner and she keeps them warm.
neath her wings they sleep 'till a - no - ther day is here.

Riqui Ran

Spanish

Ri - qui, ri - qui, ri - qui ran en el

bos - que de San Juan, vue - lan las a - be - jas cer - ca, to - man

de las flo - res néc - tar, be - ben dul - ce en la en - ra - ma - da. Ri - qui,

Fiesta! Mexico and Central America © 1993 Fearon Teacher Aids

Fiesta! Mexico and Central America © 1993 Fearon Teacher Aids

Riqui Ran
English

Ri - qui, ri - qui, ri - qui ran in the for - est of San Juan. Lit - tle bees they fly a - round. Take the nec - tar from the flow - ers, sip - ping sweets in sha - dy bow - ers. Ri - qui,

Fiesta! Mexico and Central America © 1993 Fearon Teacher Aids

Canción de Cuna
Cradle Song

1. A la ro - rro ni - ño,   a la ro - rro, ro - rro, ro,
2. E- sos tus o - ji - tos,   ya los vas ce - rran - do,

que vi - ni - ste al mun - do,   só - lo por mi a - mor.
pe - ro es - tás mi - ran - do,   to - dos mis de - lei - tos.

Cradle Song
Canción de Cuna

1. Lul-la-by my lit-tle child, Lul-la, lul-la-by my love.
2. Lit-tle eyes that are so bright, You must close them soft-ly now.

You who came in-to this world on-ly through my love.
Close them, sweet, but still you'll see all of my de-lights.

El Tambor de la Alegría
The Drum of Joy

Pana - me - ño, Pa - na - me - ño, Pa - na - me - ño, no te tar - des. Ven

pron - to va - mos jun - tos, a don-de to - can los tam - bor - es. Es - cucha el

rit - mo pum, pum, pum pum. ¿Sa- bes lo que el - los di - cen? Ven

pron - to va - mos jun - tos a don-de to - can los tam - bor - es.

Fiesta! Mexico and Central America © 1993 Fearon Teacher Aid.

The Drum of Joy
El Tambor de la Alegría

Pana - me - ño, Pa - na - me - ño, Pa - na - me - ño, no de - lay - ing. Come

quick - ly we'll go to - geth - er where the drums of joy are play - ing! Hear the

rhythm go boom, boom, boom, boom. Do you know what they are say-ing? Come

quick-ly, we'll go to - geth - er where the drums of joy are play-ing!

Niño Querido

Dearest Child

1. Ni - ño que - ri - do, duér - me - te ya,
2. Los pa - ja - ri - llos duer - men tam - bién,

que mien - tras tan - to te can - ta ma - má.
mien - tras sus pa - dres bus - can de co - mer.

Dearest Child
Niño Querido

1. Child that I love, now close your bright eyes,
2. All the small birds are al - so a - sleep, while

Ma - ma will sing you a lul - la - by.
Ma - ma and Pa - pa find good things to eat.

Fiesta! Mexico and Central America © 1993 Fearon Teacher Aids

La Piñata
The Piñata

Ándale niño no pierdas el tino. Que de la distancia se pierde el camino. Con los ojos bien vendados, En las manos un bas-

tón. Ya se rom-pe la pi - ña-ta sin te-ner-le com - pa - sión:

¡Dá le, dá-le, dá - le! no pier-das el ti - no que de la dis-

tan-cia se pier-de el ca-mi-no. ¡Dá le, dá-le,

The Piñata
La Piñata

Come a-long chil-dren and take your aim ear-ly.

When you swing at the pi-ña-ta you must hit sure-ly.

On your eyes we'll put a blind - fold. In your hands a bat to

swing. Soon we'll break the gay pi - ña - ta with no

mer - cy for the thing. Come a - long and

Para Quebrar la Piñata

Breaking the Piñata

En las no-ches de po-sa-da la pi-ña-ta es lo me-jor. La ni-ña más re-mil-

ga – da se al – bo – ro – ta con ar – dor.

Dá – le, dá – le, dá – le no pier – das el

ti – no que de la dis – tan – cia se pier – de el ca – mi – no.

Breaking the Piñata
Para Quebrar la Piñata

On the nights that are po - sa - da, there are plea - sures for the child, but the best is the pi -

Fiesta! Mexico and Central America © 1993 Fearon Teacher Aids

ña - ta, all the boys and girls go wild!

For your blow to break it you must guess the

dis - tance, not ev' - ry - one will make it, you must have per - sis - tence!

El Coquí
The Croaker

Fiesta! Mexico and Central America © 1993 Fearon Teacher Aids

The Croaker
El Coquí

qui, co - quí, co - quí, quí, quí, quí; Co - quí, co -
quí, co - quí, quí, quí, quí.

Fine

1. Oh the song of the
2. As I lie in my

Fiesta! Mexico and Central America © 1993 Fearon Teacher Aids

frog is en - chant - ing,
bed in the ev'n - ing, his voice is so clear and so
the

sweet.

frog sings me soft - ly to sleep.

Dal Segno al Fine

Arre, Caballito

Get Along, My Pony

1. ¡A - rre, ca - ba -
2. ¡A - rre, ca - ba -

lli - to! Va - mos a Be - lén,
lli - to! ¡A - rre, a - rre, a - rre!

que ma - ña - na es fies - ta, pa - sa - do tam -
¡A - rre, ca - ba - lli - to! Que lle - ga - mos

Fiesta! Mexico and Central America © 1993 Fearon Teacher Aids

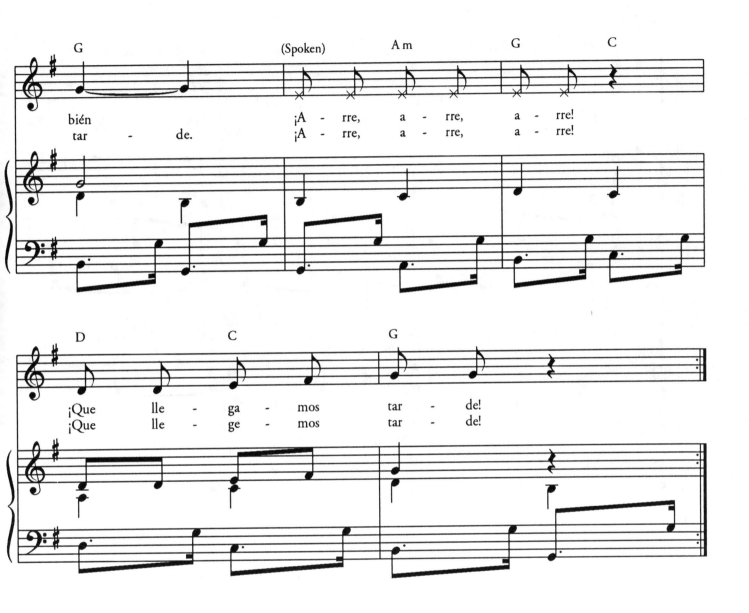

bién tar - de.
¡A - rre, a - rre, a - rre!
¡A - rre, a - rre, a - rre!

¡Que lle - ga - mos tar - de!
¡Que lle - ge - mos tar - de!

Get Along, My Pony

Arre, Caballito

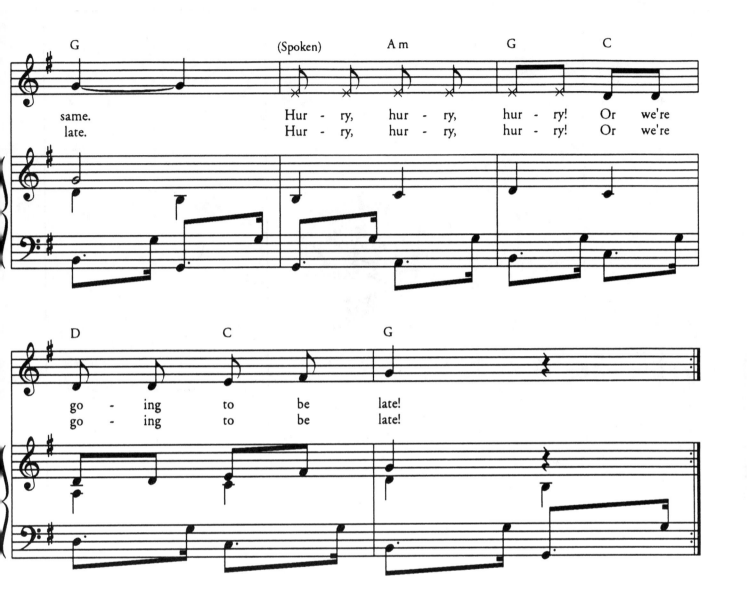

Costa Rican Flag

Fiesta! Mexico and Central America 1993 © Fearon Teacher Aids

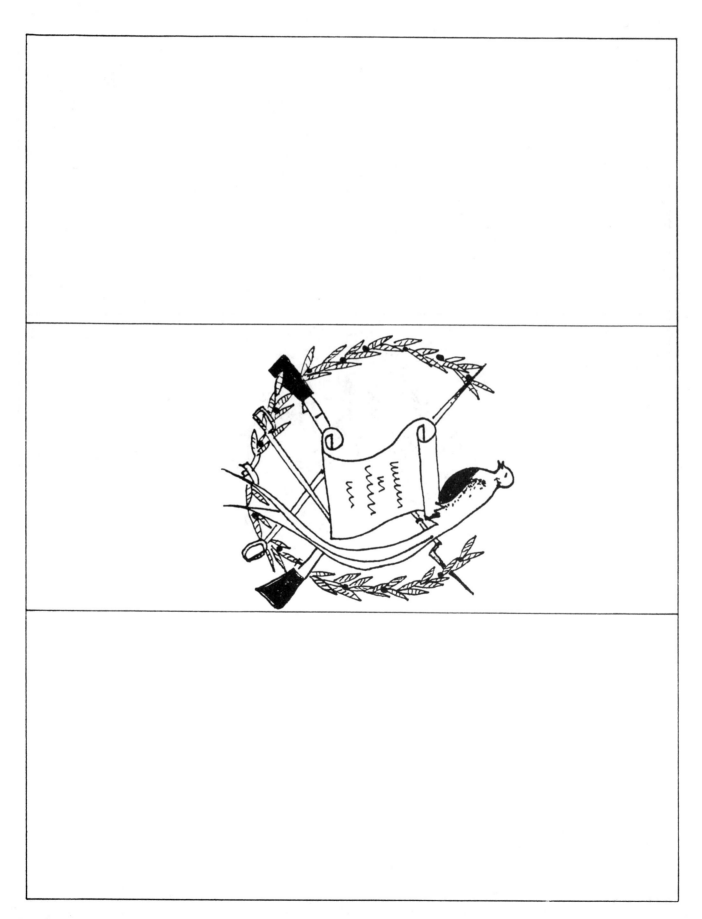

Fiesta! Mexico and Central America 1993 © Fearon Teacher Aids

Mexican Flag

Panamanian Flag

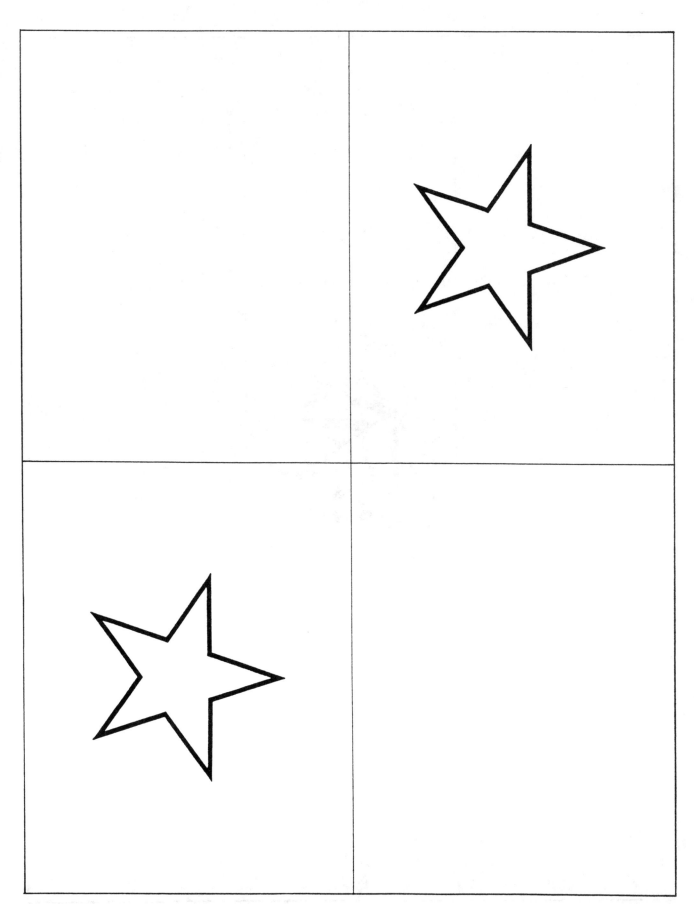

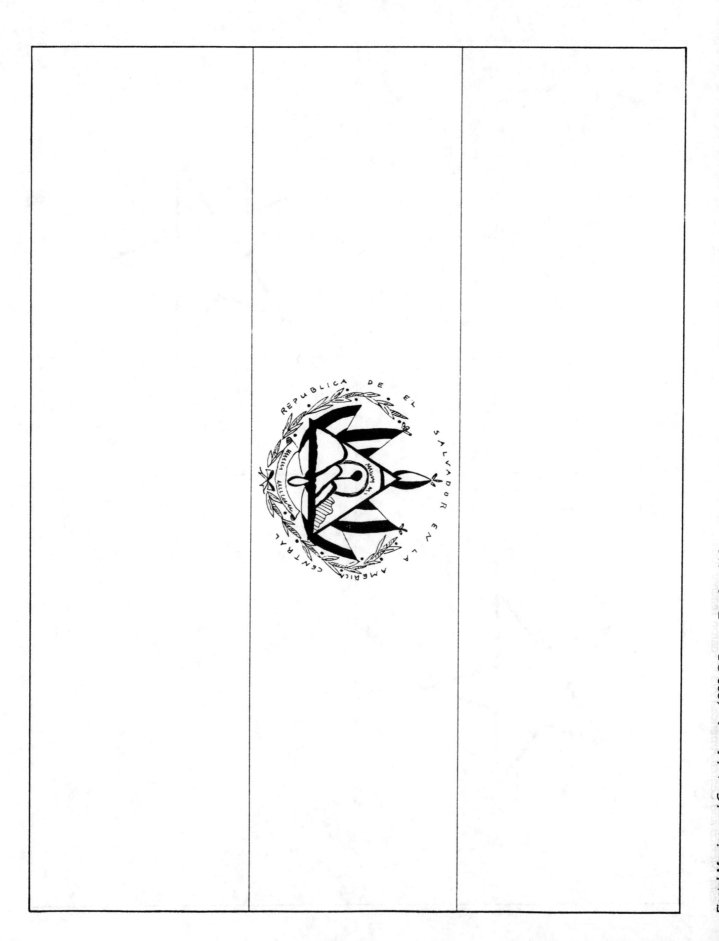

Central American Map

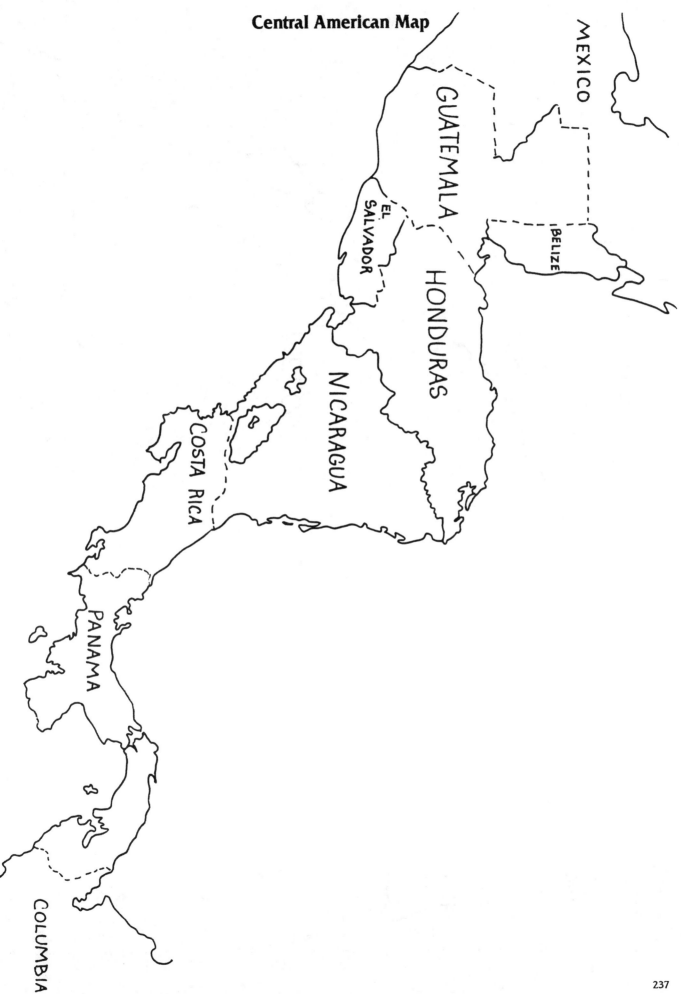

MEXICO

GUATEMALA

EL SALVADOR

BELIZE

HONDURAS

NICARAGUA

COSTA RICA

PANAMA

COLUMBIA

Mexican Map

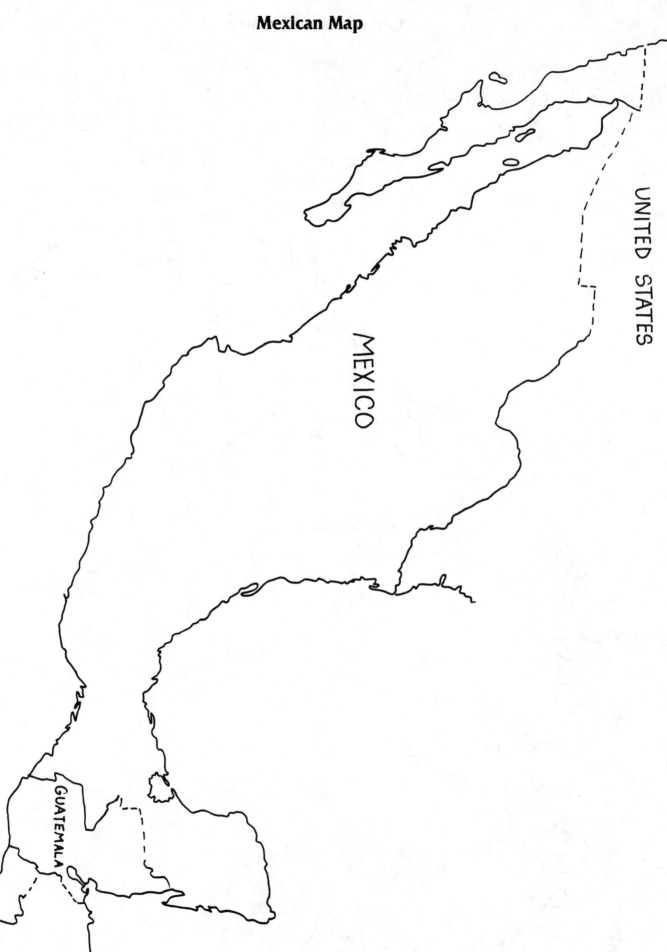

UNITED STATES

MEXICO

GUATEMALA

Bibliography

In this section, you will find lists of books, records, tapes, and community resources to help expand your and the children's enjoyment of discovering more about Mexico and Central America.

MEXICO AND CENTRAL AMERICAN BOOKS

The following books will be enjoyed by children and adults alike. You may wish to add some of the titles to your professional library.

A Treasury of Mexican Folkways by Frances Toor. New York, NY: Crown, 1987.

The Adventures of Connie and Diego by Connie Garcia. San Francisco, CA: Children's Book Press, 1987.

Americas by Sheila Fairfield. Milwaukee, WI: Gareth Stevens, Inc., 1988.

Ancient America by Marian Wood. New York, NY: Equinox Books, 1991.

The Ancient Mayan by Barbara Beck. New York, NY: Franklin Watts, 1983.

Aztecs and Spaniards by Albert Marrin. New York, NY: Franklin Watts, 1986.

The Bells of Santa Lucia by Morgan Cazzola. New York, NY: Philomel, 1991.

Brother Anansi and the Cattle Ranch by James de Sauza. San Francisco, CA: Children's Book Press, 1989.

Cortez and the Aztec Conquest by Irwin Blacker. New York, NY: American Heritage, 1965.

The Day of the Dead by Chloe Sayers. Austin, TX: University of Texas Press, 1991.

The Fall of the Aztecs by Shirley Glubok. New York, NY: St. Martin's Press, 1965.

Family Pictures by Carmen Graza. San Francisco, CA: Children's Book Press, 1989.

Famous Mexican Americans by Janet Morey and Wendy Dunn. New York, NY: Cobblehill Books, 1989.

Fire and Blood by T. R. Fehrenbach. New York, NY: Macmillan, 1972.

The First Book of the Incas by Barbara Beck. San Francisco, CA: Children's Book Press, 1966.

Fodor's Central America by Deborah Bernardi. New York, NY: Fodor's Travel Publications, 1987.

Folk Art Traditions II: The Day of the Dead by Bobbie Salinas Norman. Oakland, CA: Piñata Publications, 1989.

The Golden Coin by Alma Ada. New York, NY: Atheneum, 1991.

The History of Mexico by Henry Parkes. Boston, MA: Houghton Mifflin, 1966.

The House on Mango Street by Sandra Cisneros. New York, NY: Vintage Books, 1989.

The Invisible Hunters by Harriet Rohmer, Octavio Chow, and Morries Vidaure. San Francisco, CA: Children's Book Press, 1987.

The Legend of El Dorado: A Latin American Tale by Beatriz Vidal. New York, NY: Knopf, 1991.

The Legend of Food Mountain by Rea Rohmer. San Francisco, CA: Children's Book Press, 1988.

Magic Dogs of the Volcanoes: A Salvadoran Story by Argueta Ross. San Francisco, CA: Children's Book Press, 1990.

Lupita Manana by Patricia Beatty. New York, NY: William Morrow and Co., 1981.

Maya, Aztecs, and Inca Pop-Up Book by Duncan Birmingham. San Francisco, CA: Children's Book Press, 1984.

The Mexican Story by May McNeer. Winchester, OH: Ariel Press, 1953.

Mexico Is People: Land of Three Cultures by Barbara Nolen. New York, NY: Scribner's Sons, 1973.

My Aunt Otilla's Spirits by Richard Garcia. San Francisco, CA: Children's Book Press, 1987.

The Panama Canal: Gateway to the World by Judith St. George. New York, NY: Putnam Berkley Publishing Group, 1989.

Passport to Mexico by Carmen Irizarry. New York, NY: Franklin Watts, 1987.

The People's Guide to Mexico by Lorena Havens. Sante Fe, NM: John Muir Publications, 1986.

Pepito's Story by Gene Fern. New York, NY: Yarrow, 1991.

Pyramid of the Sun and the Moon by Leonard Fischer. New York, NY: Macmillan, 1988.

The Rise and Fall of the Maya Civilization by J. Eric Thompson. Norman, OK: University of Oklahoma Press, 1966.

Salinas Norman's ABC's and Folk Art Traditions 1 and 2 by Bobbi Salinas Norman. Oakland, CA: Piñata Publications, 1988.

The Sun Kingdom of the Aztecs by Victor von Hagen. Cleveland, OH: World Publishing, 1958.

Take a Trip to Central America by Keith Lye. New York, NY: Scholastic, 1990.

Take a Trip to Panama by John Griffith. New York, NY: Franklin Watts, 1989.

Tales from Silver Lands by Charles Finger. New York, NY: Franklin Watts, 1983.

The Thunder King: A Latin American Story by Amanda Loveseed. San Francisco, CA: Children's Book Press, 1990.

La Visita del Sr. Azucar by Rea Rohmer. San Francisco, CA: Children's Book Press, 1989.

The Woman Who Outshone the Sun by Rosalma Zubizarreta-Ada, et al. San Francisco, CA: Children's Book Press, 1991.

MEXICAN AND CENTRAL AMERICAN MUSIC BOOKS AND RECORDS

Arroz con Leche by Lulu Delacre. New York, NY: Scholastic.

The Mexican Psaltery. New York, NY: Peters International.

Vamos a Cantar by Corvalan. New York, NY: Folkways Records.

MEXICAN AND CENTRAL AMERICAN COOKBOOKS

The Cuisines of Mexico by Diana Kennedy. New York, NY: Harper & Row, 1975.

Mexican Cook Book. Des Moines, IA: Better Homes and Gardens, 1986.

The Tortilla Book and Recipes from the Regional Cooks of Mexico by Diana Kennedy. New York, NY: Harper & Row, 1975.

MEXICAN AND CENTRAL AMERICAN ARTS AND CRAFTS BOOKS

The Art of the Folk: Mexican Heritage Through Arts and Crafts for Boys and Girls by Barbara Linse. Larkspur, CA: Art's Publications, 1980.

Crafts of Mexico by Chloe Sayer. New York, NY: Doubleday and Co., Inc., 1977.

Folk Art of the Americas by August Panyella. New York, NY: Harry N. Abrams, Inc., 1981.

Mexican Folk Toys, Festival Decorations, and Ritual Objects by Florence and Robert Pettit. Mamaroneck, NY: Hastings House Publisher, 1976.